The LITTLE BOOK of
Cakes
& Bakes

First edition printed in 2019 in the UK.

ISBN: 978-1-910863-48-0

Edited by: Katie Fisher, Phil Turner

Designed by: Paul Cocker

Compiled by: Anna Tebble

Photography by: Tim Green, Marc
Barker, Paul Cocker, Matt Crowder, Carl
Sudonik, Paul Carrol, Sam Bowles

Contributors: Sarah Koriba,
David Wilson, Vanesa Balaj,
Ruth Alexander, Amelia Brownhill

me:ze
PUBLISHING

Published by Meze Publishing Limited

Unit 1b, 2 Kelham Square

Kelham Riverside

Sheffield S3 8SD

Web: www.mezepublishing.co.uk

Telephone: 0114 275 7709

Email: info@mezepublishing.co.uk

Contents

Welcome to
The Little Book Of Cakes & Bakes

We have scoured the UK for the best artisan producers, charming cafés, bakeries, tearooms, farm shops and many more unique ventures in our 'Get Stuck In' series of regional cook books. The recipes they have produced make up a glorious collection that's too good not to share!

So we have brought the most mouth-watering cakes and tempting bakes together from all across the country, celebrating the talent and knowledge of people who do this for a living with pride and passion.

From the north east to the south west, this book showcases regional specialities, classics, contemporary creations and more from independent businesses large and small. In addition to their recipes and stories, you'll find helpful extras including tips and tricks for mastering that elusive perfect rise or golden crust, and a glossary of baking terminology to decode any confusing bakers' lingo.

Whether you're a novice in the kitchen or a keen experimenter, this book is one to learn from and be inspired by, a go-to compilation for impressing your friends, baking with your kids and treating your other half (or yourself, of course) to a little bit of indulgence.

Featuring naughty-but-nice treats such as Mill Kitchen's Raspberry Cheesecake Brownie, showstoppers like Jasmin's Toffee Apple Cake from Homemade, and impressive pastry including Slattery's Manchester Tart, The Little Book of Cakes and Bakes has a sweet treat for every occasion.

We hope you love this new collection of recipes and stories as much as we do!

Tips And Tricks

We've worked with some true baking aficionados over the years, and picked up a few pearls of wisdom along the way. Whether passed down through the generations in a family business, or discovered by innovation and experimentation, these titbits make creating magic in the kitchen that much easier. Have fun, get great results, and enjoy the process!

Start with the right equipment

Having the right baking equipment in your kitchen will help you execute recipes as planned and keep baking disasters at bay. Every household is on a different budget, but you can make most bakes with a set of scales, a wooden spoon, a mixing bowl and a cake tin. Thin and flimsy tins and tray won't conduct heat evenly, so it's worth investing in a few good quality cookware essentials that will prove reliable and last you a lifetime. Some of the equipment you might want to buy includes: a large metal or glass mixing bowl, measuring spoons, a balloon whisk, a palette knife, a spatula, various sizes and shapes of cake tins and baking trays, a sieve, rolling pin, pastry brush and biscuit cutters.

Get organised

Read the recipe carefully before you begin to ensure that you have enough time to make it (don't forget about any preparation time) and that you have all the required ingredients and equipment to hand. You don't want to be nipping to the shop halfway through!

Use fresh ingredients

Unlike many of this book's contributors, who grow their own fruit or mill their own flour, you might not have easy access to ingredients straight from the field or the farm. But do use fresh free-range eggs where possible, buy locally grown fruit at its prime in season and check your cupboards for out-of-date baking essentials. You might be surprised to know that flour and baking powder have a fairly short shelf life, which could mean that your bakes won't rise as well. Fresh flour should be smooth, not chalky, and bicarbonate of soda should fizz when added to an acidic liquid such as vinegar or lemon juice. Check that eggs haven't gone off by gently placing them in a bowl of water; if the egg sinks, it's fine, but if it floats don't use it.

Think about temperature

Generally, when creaming butter with sugar, the butter should be at room temperature in order to combine smoothly. The same goes for eggs in most cases. However, when making pastry your ingredients should be kept as cold as possible, so always check the recipe and make sure your ingredients are at the specified temperature before use for the best results.

Weigh accurately

Digital scales are a very useful gadget to have in the kitchen. Baking is a precise art and you'll need the help of modern technology to ensure your measurements are exact and your cakes delicious. A cup of flour varies from one household to the next, but the scales never lie! Make sure that you weigh all dry ingredients such as flour, sugar and cocoa powder before you sieve them, unless the recipe states otherwise.

Preheat the oven

The first step of any recipe that requires the use of an oven will probably instruct you to preheat it; don't ignore this! The oven should be at just the right temperature before the bake goes in.

Pay attention to techniques and equipment

Beating, folding and creaming are just some of the terms that can easily confuse a novice baker, but they describe distinct processes that can often make the difference between a successful bake and a failed one. See our handy glossary on page 186 if you come across a term you're unsure about. Equally important are the correct utensils; trying to whisk with a spatula or fold with a balloon whisk would prove very tricky!

Substitute with care

Some recipes offer alternative options so you can personalise bakes to your own taste and preference but, for the most part, every ingredient used in a recipe serves a purpose beyond taste – colour, texture, moisture – so it's important to know what you're doing when you swap white sugar for brown or butter for oil. Experience is the best teacher when it comes to personalising your bakes.

Get to know your oven

Watch out for any hotspots in your oven, and remember that baking times may be longer or shorter depending on the accuracy of your oven thermometer. If you are unsure of where the best cooking spot is in your oven, place your bake in the centre on the middle shelf and rotate halfway through the cooking time to avoid an uneven finish.

Don't overcrowd

Try not to put too many bakes in the oven at the same time as there needs to be a good circulation of air for them to cook properly. This also applies to cookies or biscuits on a baking tray; they will usually spread out during baking and need space to expand. If you're baking a larger quantity than specified in the recipe you're following, you will need to extend cooking times accordingly.

How to check your bake is done

Checking that your bake is done is a crucial part of the cooking process, but try not to open the oven door during the first stages of baking. Doing so will allow heat to escape and temperature to drop, which will in turn affect baking time and texture. When the given cooking time is up, you can check your bake in several ways. For lighter sponges, use your fingertip to gently press the centre of the cake. If the sponge springs back into shape, it's ready; if you leave a dent, put the cake back in the oven for a few minutes. For richer cakes and bakes, you can use the trusty skewer method: poke a skewer into the centre of the bake, and if it comes out clean you are ready to go, but if not, it needs a few more minutes. For pastry, looks alone are normally enough, as properly baked pastry should be a lovely golden-brown colour.

Don't forget cooling time

Whether at room temperature or in the refrigerator, when a recipe calls for you to cool a bake it's to give it time to set. This will make handling the bake easier, allow you to get a more precise finish when decorating, and ensure the texture of the finished product is just right. So be patient and follow the cooling instructions; your bake will thank you for it!

Wait to decorate

Make sure your bake has cooled completely before decorating, so icings and glazes don't melt and run off. An apricot glaze, made from warmed and sieved apricot jam, makes a good first coating for a cake before you ice it. This stops any crumbs from getting into the icing and ensures the cake won't absorb its moisture, so your icing will stay nice and glossy.

Be proud of your bake

Baking is all about having fun and creating a (hopefully) delicious bake to enjoy with whoever you choose to share it. Of course, baking doesn't always go exactly to plan, so don't be disheartened if it doesn't turn out how you expected! What matters is that you tried and next time you know what not to do. So whether your bake is a complete disaster or a stupendously beautiful masterpiece, be proud of your bake!

AHH TOOTS

Irresistible Cakes Toot Sweet!

A small independent cakery in the heart of St Nicholas Market, Ahh Toots is the place where art and cake come together for truly irresistible results…

By day, Ahh Toots is best-known as a busy little café dishing up the type of breakfasts that have people queuing up day after day; sizzling free-range bacon is served in crusty white doorstep slices of bread. Lunch options are piled high from 12pm, including fresh free-range sausage rolls ready to be devoured, and there are plenty of vegan and gluten-free offerings, too.

However, you may be distracted before you get to the counter… the old Victorian cart laden with the most stunning cakes in the city has passersby standing in awe. From indulgent banana bread dripping with salted caramel to intricate cakes that are decorative works of art, it is clear that owner Tamarind is a firm believer in "eating with your eyes" before taking that first delicious bite.

AHH TOOTS
4-8 Glass Arcade
St Nicholas
Market
Bristol BS1 1LJ

Telephone:
01179559358
Website:
www.ahhtoots.
co.uk

Art-focussed
cakery in the heart
of Bristol. Find us
on Instagram @
ahhtoots.

Tamarind had always worked in kitchens. She grew up in a little bed and breakfast where her mum had her helping out with catering from the age of 12. Surrounded by a love of food and gifted with natural creativity, it is no surprise that she progressed towards baking, where she could indulge in dramatic designs and artistic creations. With a degree in Fine Art under her belt, Tamarind has successfully brought her joint passions together to create some truly stunning bespoke cakes. She has been involved in some impressive collaborations, including Young British Foodie events at The Tate Britain.

One of the things Tamarind most enjoys is creating individual celebration cakes for people, be it for a wedding, a party or an event. She loves developing flavour combinations and striving to create something new and original that will excite all the senses. Having recently expanded the business and taken on her own private bakery, cakes to order from Ahh Toots are flourishing, all available to buy and browse on the website.

There is something a little bit magical about Ahh Toots according to its many fans, who visit the quirky venue in the hustle and bustle of the market. Perhaps it's those standalone beautiful cakes, perhaps it's the commitment to ethical suppliers and local produce, perhaps it's those mouth-watering sausage rolls that have become renowned at their tea rooms… or perhaps it's simply being part of that whole vibrant market experience where food, creativity and community come together so seamlessly.

Ahh Toots
The Devil's Food Cake

This has to be a firm favourite on the cart and a show stopper to say the least. It's rich, fudgy, indulgent, oozing with salted caramel – and the more decorations the better – plus it's easier to make than you might think!

PREPARATION TIME: 30-45 MINUTES | BAKING TIME: 30-40 MINUTES | SERVES: 15-20

INGREDIENTS
For the cake:
500g caster sugar
100g cocoa powder
500ml boiling water
450g plain flour
1 tsp bicarbonate of soda
1 tsp baking powder
Good pinch of salt
250g butter
4 medium eggs

For the filling and icing:
400g unsalted butter
650g icing sugar
1 tin of Carnation caramel

For the glaze:
125g butter
1 dessert spoon of maple syrup
200g dark chocolate

To decorate:
The baker's favourites are chocolate shards, popcorn, chocolate bars, pretzels...or whatever takes your fancy!

METHOD

Grease and line three 8cm by 20cm round cake tins. Preheat the oven to 170°c.

For the cake mixture, first make the hot chocolate in a jug by combining 200g of the caster sugar with the cocoa powder and boiling water. Stir until smooth. Sieve the flour and raising agents into a bowl with the salt, and use an electric mixer with a separate bowl to cream the butter and the remaining 300g of caster sugar. Continue to mix while you add the eggs one at a time, each with a spoonful of the flour mixture to stop the wet ingredients splitting. Once the eggs are incorporated, add the remaining flour mixture and the hot chocolate in thirds, mixing thoroughly and scraping down the bowl between each addition. Once you have a smooth cake batter, divide it evenly between the prepared tins.

Bake the cakes for 30 minutes in the preheated oven. Check if they are done by inserting a skewer or thin knife into the centre; if it comes out clean the sponge is done. Leave to cool. Meanwhile, in an electric mixer or by hand (good luck) beat the butter and icing sugar together until white and fluffy (this can take 20 minutes) to make the butter icing. When the cakes are completely cool, place one on a cake plate, lather with a thick layer of caramel (leaving a 2cm gap around the edge) followed by a good layer of butter icing. Smooth out with a palette knife and repeat with the other two layers.

To crumb coat the cake, gently pull a thin layer of butter icing around the edges of the cake using a palette knife. Set a little in the fridge, then repeat to get a nice smooth layer of icing. Set again and put the remaining butter icing in a piping bag. Spread some caramel around the outside of the cake and place back in the fridge. For that all-important drip, make a glaze by melting the butter, syrup and chocolate together in a bain-marie. Stir until smooth then leave to cool slightly. Pour the glaze into the centre of the cake, leave for a minute and then tease just over the edges using a palette knife or the back of a spoon to get the desired drip effect. Leave to set.

Now comes the fun part! Pipe the remaining butter icing onto the set glaze in whatever design takes your fancy, and decorate however you see fit. We use lots of chocolate; my faves are Mars Bars, loads of popcorn and always pretzels.

"I love developing flavour combinations and striving to create something new and original that will excite all the senses."

Tamarind, founder, Ahh Toots

THE ALPHABET GIFT SHOP

Easy as A,B,C

The Alphabet Gift Shop is a thriving business on a mission to surprise and delight with beautifully made, personalised products and freshly prepared food & drink.

THE ALPHABET GIFT SHOP BURTON

9-10 Union Street
Burton-on-Trent
Staffordshire
DE14 1AA
Telephone:
01283 749933

THE ALPHABET GIFT SHOP MICKLEOVER

44 Station Road
Mickleover
Derby
DE3 9GH
Telephone:
01332 513033
Website:
www.thealphabet
giftshop.co.uk

Two gift shops with a wide selection of beautifully made, carefully chosen, design-led products which can be personalised at the Burton studio. Each location has a coffee shop serving freshly made food, drinks and irresistible cakes throughout the day.

With food, drink, gifts, online shopping and an established reputation as a personalised gift specialist, The Alphabet Gift Shop has grown organically in response to demand from the small venture that business owner Sue began at home. The first gift shop in Mickleover in 2008 was followed by the Burton store five years later. Licensed coffee shops now nestle side by side with the gift shops in both locations, and the Burton gift shop recently extended into the shop next door.

"We have some lovely customers who have been with us since day one, and then others who have only just discovered us – all people who make it such a pleasure to run the business," says Sue.

When it comes to food and drink, both coffee bars aim to cover everyone's needs throughout the day. Visitors of all ages, even those with four legs, can be sure of a friendly welcome and a relaxed environment where artisan coffee, teas, smoothies and milkshakes can be enjoyed alongside your breakfast, brunch, lunch or afternoon tea. The kitchen uses local produce wherever possible and everything is freshly made by the chefs. Pastry chef Jo is their 'free-from' specialist who has a flair for gluten-free and vegan cakes and treats so tasty you don't even notice what's missing!

The kitchen at Mickleover has a very similar offering on a smaller scale. The cosy coffee bar is tucked behind shelves full of lovely things that Sue and the team have chosen. They are especially keen on local designers and makers, and also have their own range of bags, cushions, aprons and baby gifts which are created to allow for embroidered or printed personalisation. "If we can, we will!" says Sue with regard to making their products that little bit more special by adding a name, date or image in the studio above the Burton shop.

Growing within a network of local entrepreneurs and maintaining a family-oriented atmosphere is important to Sue, whose niece, daughter and sister all work with her at The Alphabet. The aim and ethos of the whole business is about making people and their loved ones happy through food and drink in a great place to meet, relax, and find the perfect gift.

Alphabet Gift Shop
Gluten-Free Chocolate Orange Torte

This gluten-free dessert can also be made to suit dairy-free diets by using milk-free dark chocolate and a dairy-free baking block and it's still super tasty!.

PREPARATION TIME: 20 MINUTES | BAKING TIME: 35 MINUTES | SERVES: 12

METHOD

Preheat the oven to 170°c. Grease and line a 23cm spring-form cake tin.

Melt the chocolate and butter together in a bain-marie. Remove from the heat and whisk in the orange zest and sifted cocoa. Leave to cool for about 10 minutes. Meanwhile, whisk the eggs and sugar together using an electric beater or stand mixer until pale, thick and doubled in volume. Carefully fold the chocolate mixture into the whisked egg mixture, and then pour the batter into the tin. Place in the centre of the oven on the middle shelf and bake for around 30 minutes, depending on your oven. The top will be a firmer crust and the centre will have a wobble to it. Remove from the oven and leave to cool in the tin. For easier removal, place in the fridge to finish cooling. The top will sink down and become cracked which is perfectly normal.

To serve

The torte can be served warm with crème fraîche, ice cream or a dairy-free alternative such as coconut cream. If serving the dessert cold, it can be topped with soft whipped cream and seasonal fruits for a gorgeous dinner party treat.

INGREDIENTS

225g dark chocolate, chopped
185g unsalted butter (or dairy-free baking block)
2 oranges, zested
60g cocoa powder
6 eggs
250g caster sugar

"No matter your dietary requirements, at Alphabet we make sure all bakes taste equally yummy!"

Sue, owner, The Alphabet Gift Shop

Traditional Perfection

With baking knowledge handed down from her Nan, Lucy Cassar's Apple Tree embraces traditional recipes and values with fresh modern flair.

THE APPLE TREE GIFT SHOP AND TEAHOUSE

6 Flood Street
Ockbrook
Derby
DE72 3RF

Telephone:
01332 987001
Website:
www.theappletree
giftshop.co.uk

Quintessential teahouse serving breakfast, light lunches and homemade cakes complemented by the gift shop where you can find beautiful cards, jewellery and gifts.

The Apple Tree Gift Shop and Teahouse in the village of Ockbrook has become a community hub since opening in March 2012. It even attracted the attention of chef extraordinaire Heston Blumenthal back in 2014 and has been winning awards ever since.

It's Lucy's commitment and passion for tradition and service that sets The Apple Tree apart. She strove to make her dream of owning a 'treasure trove' gift shop a reality, and sought creative ways to develop a warm, welcoming atmosphere to avoid the often clinical shop feel.

This, combined with a love of baking instilled by her Nan Joan Stafford, sparked the addition of the Apple Tree's 1950s vintage tea room. Drinks are served in good china originally donated by villagers, the tables are stained with Yorkshire Tea and an array of homemade bakes whisper enticingly to diners. Sprinkle all that with exemplary service from the passionate and humble team and you have a winning recipe.

The Apple Tree's Beautiful Breakfasts, Light Lunches and Afternoon Tea are also available and delectable cakes range from classic layer cakes, light-as-a-feather tray bakes, cookies and dietary bakes. Coffee is freshly ground as required, they have their own loose leaf tea brand, the whole menu is made fresh to order and meat is brought in from the butcher in the next village of course. The Apple Tree has become so popular that most lunchtimes are fully booked; customer demand is higher than ever.

After a fantastic feed you can be sure to enjoy a spot of shopping in their gift shop: hand finished cards, books, jewellery, candles, scarves, homeware and other treasures line the shelves. Lucy works hard to source individual, high-end items both locally and further afield, so customers can always be sure of finding a unique present.

Montage photography: Chris Towlson at infinite Symmetry

The Apple Tree
Lucy's Lemon, Lime & Raspberry Mojito Loaf

Love a mojito? We love turning cocktails into cakes, and this is our ultimate sunshine season cake that oozes summer flavours and fun. Once you've mastered the basics, you can easily adapt this recipe to any cocktail.

PREPARATION TIME: 25 MINUTES | BAKING TIME: 35-40 MINUTES | SERVES: 8-10

INGREDIENTS

For the cake:
170g margarine
170g caster sugar
3 eggs
170g self-raising flour
1 tsp baking powder
1 lemon
1 lime
Handful of frozen raspberries

For the drizzle:
½ a lemon, juiced
1 tbsp caster sugar
1 tbsp white rum

For the frosting:
100g cream cheese
50g unsalted butter
250g icing sugar
3 tbsp white rum
1 lemon
1 lime
Stem of fresh mint or edible flowers, for decoration

METHOD

Preheat the oven to 170°c.

Combine the margarine and sugar and whisk until smooth and fluffy. Gently whisk in the eggs then fold in the self-raising flour and baking powder. Grate the lemon and lime zest and add it to the cake mixture. Add the juice of one lime and crush a handful of frozen raspberries into the cake mixture then stir well. Pour the mixture into a greased and lined 2lb loaf tin then bake for 35 to 40 minutes or until a skewer can be inserted into the centre of the cake and it comes out clean.

Make the drizzle by combining the lemon juice, caster sugar and white rum.

Once out of the oven leave the cake to stand for 5 minutes then prick all over with a skewer. Drizzle the rum, sugar and lemon mixture over the top of the warm cake and leave to cool.

Finally, make the cream cheese frosting. Whisk the cream cheese, butter, icing sugar and white rum together in a bowl until you get a firm consistency. If it's too runny add more icing sugar, or if it's too solid add more cream cheese (or rum!). When you're happy with the consistency, spread the icing on the top of the loaf. We leave the icing to set before adding the finishing touches.

Cut the lemon and lime into wedges. Add these and a stem of fresh mint or some edible flowers to the top of the cake to garnish. Serve – reminding your friends it contains neat rum – and enjoy!

The Apple Tree
Gavin's Double Chocolate Fudge Brownies

This is an extremely popular choice at The Apple Tree. It's taken us three years of experimenting to perfect the recipe and it's incredibly rewarding when our customers can't believe this gooey brownie is gluten-free! You can top the brownie with seasonal goodies such as crème eggs, mini eggs, biscuits, swirls of caramel, sprinkles... go wild!

PREPARATION TIME: 20 MINUTES | BAKING TIME: 40 MINUTES | SERVES: 9

METHOD

Preheat oven to 170°c.

Bring about two centimetres of water to a simmer in a saucepan. Place a heatproof bowl on the pan, making sure it doesn't touch the water, and put the dark chocolate, butter and a pinch of salt in the bowl. Stir until melted then remove the bowl from the heat to allow the mixture to cool.

In the meantime, whisk the eggs, brown sugar and vanilla bean extract together then add the cooled chocolate mixture to the egg mixture. Fold in the cocoa powder, flour, xanthan gum and baking powder. Roughly chop the bar of white chocolate and stir into the mixture. Pour into a greased and lined 177mm square tin and bake for 40 minutes.

Remove the brownie from the baking tin and allow to cool. For maximum fudgy texture, place in the fridge overnight. When serving cut into nine squares with a warm, sharp knife. Dust with icing sugar, et voilà!

Baker's tip: If you'd like to make this brownie, but you're not gluten intolerant, simply replace the gluten-free flour and xanthan gum with 50g of self-raising flour.

INGREDIENTS

250g dark chocolate
250g butter
A pinch of salt
4 eggs
360g dark brown sugar
2 tsp vanilla bean extract
150g cocoa powder
50g gluten-free flour
1 tsp xanthan gum
100g white chocolate
1 tsp baking powder

"Add a spoonful of love to everything you bake."

Sharon, baker, The Apple Tree

BLANCHFLOWER

Where Craft Is King

A popular artisan bakery forms the heart of Blanchflower Bakery and Kitchen's operations.

Co-founders Phil and Claire Howells describe Blanchflower as a 'working craft production centre' where the bakery and the kitchen work in harmonised unison. The venture was founded in 2017 based on a philosophy that champions meticulous attention to detail and passion for excellent food. The bakery makes sourdough bread and focaccia every day, plus all the pastry, cakes and tarts, doughnuts and viennoiserie served in the café which also does brunch and lunch.

Before Blanchflower, the husband and wife team opened one of the first speciality coffee shops in Manchester. When they went on to open the café in Longford Park, they installed a small, second hand, four tray bread oven on site. "In Manchester in 2012, it was just us and Trove making sourdough and we learned about craft production and how, through repetition and honing our craft, we learned to make the best version of something. To us, it was magical baking all our bread and cakes in the park as the sun came up every morning," says head baker Claire Howells.

"At that time, rainbow cakes were all the rage both in cafes and on the Great British Bake Off and we went hard against that. Our baking style has always been about creating big flavours with the best natural ingredients." At Blanchflower, the bakery team like to create their own versions of classic bakes. The much-loved Bakewell, for instance, contains homemade blackcurrant jam but not a hint of almond flavouring, and the drizzle cakes are always full of freshly squeezed juice.

The bakery's recipe for banana bread is a great example, with the addition of a little dark chocolate to balance the sweetness and pecans to provide some textural complexity. "It is fantastic straight from the oven, either on its own or spread with butter, and we always sell a whole loaf almost immediately that they come out as they smell so amazing," says Claire. "We sell it mainly toasted in Longford Park and on its own at Blanchflower, so that proves it works both ways."

BLANCH FLOWER

12-14 Shaw's Road
Altrincham
WA14 1QU

Telephone:
0161 929 6724

Website:
www.
blanchflower.co

Artisan bakery
and restaurant
where everything
is made in-house.

BLANCH FLOWER
KITCHEN & BAKERY

Blanchflower
Banana Bread with Chocolate & Pecans

"We wanted to share this recipe because it's an absolute South Manchester classic which has been eaten by literally thousands of our customers. It's relatively easy to bake at home and is amazing warm straight from the oven."

PREPARATION TIME: 20 MINUTES | BAKING TIME: 40-50 MINUTES | SERVES: 8

METHOD

Preheat the oven to 180°c or 160°c fan and grease and line the bottom and sides of a 900g deep loaf tin.

Lightly toast the pecans then roughly chop. Set aside to cool.

Sift the flour together with the bicarb and salt then blend the bananas with the buttermilk and vanilla extract in an electric mixer until fairly smooth. Set the mixture aside.

Cream the butter and sugar together using an electric mixer until they are light, fluffy and pale. Gradually add the eggs, mixing well after each addition.

INGREDIENTS

30g pecans
225g plain flour
1 tsp bicarbonate of soda
½ tsp salt
3 ripe bananas, approximately 300g
60ml buttermilk
1 tsp vanilla extract
125g very soft unsalted butter
200g soft light brown sugar
2 eggs
40g dark chocolate chips
Demerara sugar, to sprinkle

Once combined gradually add the banana mixture and the flour mixture alternately on a low speed, mixing only until just combined. Don't worry if the mixture starts to look a little curdled after each banana addition.

Finally add the chopped pecans and chocolate chips and lightly combine. Scrape the mixture into the prepared loaf tin, level and then sprinkle liberally with Demerara sugar until lightly covered. This will give the loaf a nice shiny, cracked top.

Bake the loaf in the preheated oven for approximately 40 to 50 minutes until a skewer comes out clean. Allow to cool in the tin for about 15 minutes, then turn out and serve.

"It's magical baking all our bread and cakes in the park as the sun comes up every morning."

Claire, head baker, Blanchflower

BONDGATE BAKERY

Baking The Old-Fashioned Way

Back in 1984, Steve Taylor had one issue on his mind: no matter how hard he looked he couldn't find good, real bread anywhere. So he decided to bake it himself!

BONDGATE
BAKERY
30 Bondgate
Otley
LS21 1 AD

Telephone:
01943 467516

Website:
www.
bondgatebakery.
com

Baking bread
the traditional
way since 1984.
Bondgate Bakery
makes all its
products on site
from family
recipes.

Everything Bondgate Bakery sell is made on-site, from scratch. From their traditional bread and Yorkshire curd tarts, brownies and parkin to quiches and hummus, there are no additives, preservatives or factory-made mixes in anything. Sally, Steve's wife, explains: "It's really important to us that our raw ingredients are pure and unadulterated. That has been our motto since we first started in 1984 and it will never change."

The small market town of Otley welcomed Bondgate Bakery into the community 32 years ago and Sally could not be more grateful: "Otley has a mix of people from all walks of life and our shop took off straight away; the people really welcomed us. In turn, we try to cater for everyone here, with a wide range of products including numerous gluten-free breads and also healthier bakes such as low sugar cakes. We've built up strong links with our local suppliers and this fuels the community spirit here! It feels good to work together with other local businesses."

Bondgate now employ five bakers and their shop and wholesale business has expanded year on year, but their classic curd tarts are still made according to Steve's grandmother's recipe and so is their flapjack. With traditional bakes made excellently, you can be sure whatever you purchase from this bakery is made with love. Of course, their traditionally baked bread is the bestseller. Breadmaking is an ancient art, one which the team at Bondgate have spent years perfecting. From wholemeal and seeded varieties to rye and sourdough, Steve and his bakers spend hours every day making each loaf. The slow fermentation process means nutrients and flavour are locked in for that comforting, home-baked taste every time.

With all the right ingredients for success, it comes as no surprise that Bondgate Bakery have been recognised with awards both locally and nationally. Winning 'Best Small Retailer' at the BBC Food and Farming Awards brought the bakery lots of publicity and they have also won 'Best Bakery in the UK' in the Farm Shop and Deli Awards. Sally is really proud: "It's really so rewarding to be recognised on a national scale by our industry peers." With accolades rolling in from locals and industry professionals alike, it's clear that this bakery will continue to build on its already well-established reputation, with a long and bright future ahead.

Bondgate Bakery
Fruity Frangipani Tray Bake

This simple but tasty sponge is gluten-free thanks to the use of ground almonds instead of flour, which also give the cake a lovely moist texture. Choose any fruit you like that's in season; the versatility makes this a great year-round treat.

PREPARATION TIME: 15 MINUTES | BAKING TIME: 25-30 MINUTES | SERVES: 8

METHOD
Line a medium-sized baking tin and preheat the oven to 200°c.

Make sure the butter has been taken out the fridge to soften. Whisk the eggs and caster sugar together until the mixture is full of air and thick, then gently add the butter, a little at a time. Fold in the ground almonds, taking care not to knock out too much air.

Pour the cake batter into the prepared baking tin and sprinkle the fruit over to distribute evenly. Bake until firm and a skewer comes out cleanly from the centre. Leave to cool in the tin.

Once completely cool, remove the cake from the tin, dust with icing sugar and slice into portions.

INGREDIENTS
180g free-range eggs
220g caster sugar
150g butter, softened
240g ground almonds
150-200g fruit of your choice (soft summer fruits like peaches or any kind of berry would work)

"It's really important to us that our raw ingredients are pure and unadulterated. That has been our motto since we first started in 1984 and it will never change."

Sally, co-owner, Bondgate Bakery

THE BRIDGE BAKEHOUSE

Sisters Doing It For Themselves

Sisters Camilla and Courtney started out by selling homemade treats during their childhood summer holidays, and have come full circle to run their own bakery and shop in Whaley Bridge.

THE BRIDGE BAKEHOUSE
42A Market Street
Whaley Bridge
High Peak
Derbyshire
SK23 7LP

Telephone:
01663 734113

Website: www.
thebridge
bakehouse.co.uk

The Bridge Bakehouse is a beautiful family-run artisan patisserie and is the pride and joy of Whaley Bridge, Derbyshire.

The Bridge Bakehouse is a happy combination of its owners' home town and family. Camilla Dignan runs Whaley Bridge's much-loved independent bakery and shop with her sister Courtney Dignan. While Courtney looks after the retail side of things, Camilla, along with her team of talented bakers, creates a blend of classic British favourites and fine French patisserie to be delivered each morning for both wholesale and café customers. Her mum and dad are also involved in the business, and inspiration goes right back to the sisters' Nana with whom they learnt to bake while visiting her in Wales, and would then set up cake stalls to treat other holidaymakers to their efforts!

Before embarking on The Bridge Bakehouse journey, Camilla was a pastry chef with experience of working in high-end restaurants – including Fischers in Baslow – and the Young Pastry Chef of the Year title to her name. Today she enjoys working with local businesses, particularly the Spar in Calver, Derbyshire which was one of her first partnerships and still has the biggest range of products. Wholesale is a mostly local affair, but also supplies the second largest garden centre in the country, Bents in Lancashire.

The lucky residents of Whaley Bridge can pop by Courtney's shop whenever they fancy a treat or a takeaway lunch. Coffees, teas, sandwiches, savoury bakes and cakes are available during the day from the café to be enjoyed under the awning; the outdoor seating is always occupied even when it's snowing! Local recommendation has been important to Camilla, who is still adding to her repertoire as she experiments with new trends and flavours alongside the well-known favourites. "We try to provide something for everyone," she says, "and most people do say 'wow' when they see the counter, and some take half an hour to choose what they want!"

The sisters recently came up with a new feature to solve this dilemma; selection boxes allow customers to try a little of everything. They also take their treats to farmers' markets and other local events including Chatsworth Christmas Market, and have thought about the possibility of other shops but like to keep the business small and personal. For Camilla and Courtney it's all about making the things they love to eat, so continuing to create great bakes is top of the agenda!

Bridge Bakehouse Lemon Meringue Pie

Our classic lemon meringue pie has been on our cake menu every day since we opened five years ago. If we removed it from our patisserie fridge, we guarantee there would be uproar in our usually sleepy little town of Whaley Bridge in the Peak District…

PREPARATION TIME: 30 MINUTES | BAKING TIME: 40 MINUTES |
MAKES: 6-7 INDIVIDUAL 4 INCH TARTS (10CM) OR 1 LARGE 10 INCH TART (25CM)

METHOD

For the base

We've replaced the classic sweet pastry base for a biscuit base having learnt from experience that sweet pastry can go soggy very quickly when covered with lemon curd. Our digestive base is lovely and crunchy partnered with the buttery curd and pillowy meringue. Mix the melted butter and digestive crumbs together in a bowl. Divide between six or seven individual 4 inch tart tins (or one large 10 inch tart tin.) Push down firmly on the base and up the sides with the back of a teaspoon until smooth. Chill in the fridge.

For the lemon curd

Rub the caster sugar and lemon zest together in an electric mixer with a whisk attachment (or just by hand) for 2 to 3 minutes. This releases the natural oils in the zest. It should smell lemony and aromatic. Whisk in the eggs, then the lemon juice. Place in a medium-sized heavy-bottomed saucepan on a medium to high heat and whisk constantly until the mixture reaches 80°c on a kitchen thermometer. Pass through a sieve using the back of a ladle and leave to cool to 60°c. We normally put ours in the fridge for 5 to 10 minutes. When cool, blend the curd with a stick blender or in a food processor while gradually adding the butter cubes, a little at a time. When combined, the lemon curd is ready! Pour into the biscuit crumb lined tin (or tins) and smooth over with the back of a spoon. Chill in the fridge for at least one hour, but longer would be better.

For the Italian meringue

In a medium-size bowl, whisk together the egg whites and caster sugar until just combined. Place over a pan of simmering water and heat to 50°c, whisking occasionally. Once the mixture has reached 50°c whisk and whip until the mixture is soft, glossy and holds a firm peak.

To assemble

Remove the tarts from their tins and place on a plate or cake stand. Fill a piping bag with the meringue and pipe 'blobs' over the lemon curd filling. Alternatively, scoop the meringue on with a spoon and roughly make swirls with a fork. Using a cook's blowtorch, gently toast the meringue, being careful not to burn the tops. You can place the pies under a hot grill if you don't have a blowtorch, but watch the meringue very carefully to just brown it. Serve and enjoy!

INGREDIENTS

For the base

330g butter, melted
425g digestive biscuits, finely crushed

For the lemon curd

200g caster sugar
3 lemons, zested
4 free-range eggs
175ml lemon juice, freshly squeezed
295g unsalted butter, cubed

For the Italian meringue:

200g egg whites
400g caster sugar

"We love making people happy with our homemade sweet treats."

Camilla and Courtney, sisters and bakers,
The Bridge Bakehouse

All The Fun Of The Farm

The perfect place to spend a family day out, Bury Lane Farm Shop is a haven for anyone who enjoys fresh seasonal produce and quality choices from hot meals to cut flowers.

BURY LANE FARM SHOP
A10 Bypass
Melbourn
Royston
SG8 6DF

Telephone:
01763 260418

Website:
www.
burylane
farmshop.co.uk

Bury Lane Farm Shop offers a friendly atmosphere brought to you by a family-run team. The focus on local producers gives you a unique shopping experience.

The expression 'from field to fork' is never truer than when you browse the rows of pick your own strawberries, or choose a bunch of asparagus picked at the height of its brief season from Bury Lane Farm Shop. The farming family who own and work the land have grown their business into a veritable treasure trove of fresh and local produce.

The farm shop incorporates a delicatessen where the focus is on offering customers something a little more unusual and special, including a range of local cheeses plus cold meats, pies, quiches and fresh bread. It also boasts a butchers featuring local and rare breed meats with our sausages and burgers made on site, along with a fishmongers selling fresh fish straight from Billingsgate.

The emphasis on seasonal produce means everything that the team source for Bury Lane is at its freshest and best year-round. Along with asparagus and strawberries, they grow greenhouses full of flowers on the farm which are sold in the shop along with a large choice of fresh flowers from Covent Garden. The family make sure they support and engage with the fantastic range of suppliers and other producers around them in the Cambridgeshire countryside, reflecting the quality of the food and drink created in the area. The gift shop houses a range of cards, homeware, toys, jewellery and other treasures to explore. Bury Lane's longevity has made it a part of the community, and staff see customers returning time and again (sometimes surprised at how far things have developed since the venture's humble beginnings!).

Knowledgeable people who really care about what's being produced and sold are the cornerstone of Bury Lane. They always aim to provide visitors with an experience, not just a shopping trip, whether they're stocking up the fridge or just popping by to sample the cakes and scones which are ever-popular. Bury Lane Bakery is also owned by the family and its deliciously fresh cakes and other treats are sold in the farm shop as well as across the county in various venues.

The choice of take-home food and drink is complemented by Bury Lane's café which comfortably accommodates crowds of people for a hot lunch or breakfast. Children can also enjoy farm-themed fun in the adjoining indoor play area or head outdoors to The Beach @ Bury Lane adventure zone in the summer months. From squash to Sunday roasts, Bury Lane Farm Shop sets its sights on offering something for everyone and welcomes its visitors with plenty to explore come rain or shine.

Bury Lane Strawberry Cheesecake

Strawberry cheesecake is always a winner, and our take on this classic dessert has a lovely purée topping and makes the best use of fresh, hand-picked strawberries from our farm: from field to shop with no food miles.

PREPARATION TIME: 45 MINUTES | CHILLING TIME: 1 HOUR PLUS OVERNIGHT | SERVES: 12

METHOD

Butter and line a 23cm loose-bottomed tin with baking paper. Crush the biscuits in a plastic food bag using a rolling pin. Transfer the crumbs to a bowl, then pour over the melted butter. Mix thoroughly until the crumbs are completely coated. Tip into the prepared tin and press down firmly to create an even layer. Chill in the fridge for 1 hour to set.

Place the soft cheese, icing sugar and vanilla seeds in a bowl, then beat with an electric mixer until smooth. Tip in the cream and continue beating until combined. Spoon the cream mixture onto the biscuit base, working from the edges inwards and making sure there are no air bubbles. Smooth the top of the cheesecake down with the back of a spoon or spatula. Leave to set in the fridge overnight.

About 30 minutes before serving, bring the cheesecake to room temperature. Place the base on top of a can then gradually pull the sides of the tin down. Slip the cake onto a serving plate, removing the lining paper and base. Purée half of the strawberries in a blender or food processor with the icing sugar and 1 teaspoon of water, then sieve the purée. Pile the remaining strawberries onto the cake and pour over the purée to serve.

INGREDIENTS

250g pack of Bury Lane Salted Caramel Fudge Cookies
100g butter, melted
600g soft cheese (from our deli counter)
100g icing sugar
284ml pot double cream
1 vanilla pod, split to release seeds

For the topping:
1 punnet of Bury Lane strawberries, halved
25g icing sugar

"Seasonal and local ingredients make all the difference."

Bury Lane Farm Shop

COCORICO PATISSERIE

If The Choux Fits...

Laurian Veaudour pursued his dream to set up his own modern patisserie, where he creates delicate pastries, cakes, macarons and more to share and inspire...

COCORICO PATISSERIE

35 Whitchurch
Road
Cardiff
CF14 3JN

Telephone:
02921 328177

Website:
www.cocorico
patisserie.co.uk

Modern patisserie
creating French
delicacies and
serving freshly
made food and
drink in the café.

Pâtissier Laurian Veaudour had called Cardiff home for almost a decade when he seized the opportunity to open his own patisserie in the city. His ethos of sticking to the goals you want to achieve and discovering what suits you, rather than trying to please everyone, has resulted in a steadily growing business, and although Cocorico Patisserie has won several awards in its time, the customers who return again and again are the real measure of this success for Laurian.

Cocorico is modern, creative and driven by passionate people who aim to provide something special and different, whether for a weekend lunch or a wedding. Laurian and his two experienced pastry chefs, who also trained in France, create sweet patisserie treats in the kitchen every day. The eye-catching display counter usually includes twelve different types of cake, chocolate bonbons, traditional French delicacies with beautiful finishes and macarons in all colours and flavours. They also offer lots of options for bespoke creations to suit individual occasions, ranging from celebration cakes to classic entremets and croquembouche.

Despite the French context of the venture, when it comes to ingredients – and indeed to national identities – there are no hard and fast rules at Cocorico. Laurian considers himself half-Welsh and chooses his suppliers and staff depending on what's most suited to his style of patisserie and cooking rather than what might be classified as the best, as well as sourcing locally wherever possible. He's keen on the concept of self-sufficiency too, and already cures his own bacon and bakes sourdough bread at the café, which is used in the menus of freshly made breakfasts, lunches and afternoon teas available throughout the day.

Already host to regular pop-ups and events, Cocorico Patisserie now also offers cookery classes for those wanting to make their cake and eat it! Laurian teaches the monthly full-day introduction to patisserie himself, which provides its students with the know-how to create six different cakes (as well as lunch and more treats to take home). He wanted to set up the school because sharing skills and inspiring a younger generation is something he enjoys and hopes to do more of, having discovered that challenging yourself, meeting new people, and learning from others are the key ingredients for making a dream come true.

Cocorico Patisserie Tarte au Chocolat

This is one of my all-time favourites. Simple recipes are often the best and you can never go wrong with a good chocolate treat.

PREPARATION TIME: 15 MINUTES, PLUS 1 HOUR MINIMUM CHILLING TIME | BAKING TIME: 30 MINUTES | MAKES 12 SMALL OR 1 LARGE TARTE

METHOD

For the sweet pastry

Blend the plain flour, icing sugar and unsalted butter in a food processor until you get a sandy texture. Add the egg yolk and mix well until all the ingredients come together.

Leave for 1 hour or even better, overnight in the fridge. Roll out the pastry to 3-5mm thickness. Lay the rolled out dough in a tart case and gently mould it into the sides and base. Bake the pastry case in the oven at 150°c for 15 to 20 minutes. The case needs to cool before being filled.

For the salted caramel

Warm the whipping cream, vanilla pod and butter together in a small saucepan and then remove the vanilla pod. In another saucepan, heat 50g of the sugar then add the rest a bit at a time and keep on stirring until the sugar turns into a golden brown caramel. Add the cream mixture to the caramel along with the salt and mix until the caramel is fully dissolved. Use the mixture quickly as it will harden when cool.

For the ganache

Break the chocolate into small pieces and place in a heatproof bowl. Bring the cream to the boil and then pour it over the chocolate. Add the butter and blend using a stick blender to create a chocolate emulsion. This is now ready to use straight away.

To assemble

Pour the caramel into the tart case to form a distinct layer, and then fill the case up with ganache. Leave to set at room temperature for 2 hours for best results, and then serve and enjoy!

INGREDIENTS

For the sweet pastry:

250g plain flour
125g icing sugar
125g unsalted butter, cubed
55g egg yolk

For the salted caramel:

60g UHT whipping cream
½ vanilla pod
65g unsalted butter, cubed
150g caster sugar
4g sea salt flakes

For the chocolate ganache:

275g dark chocolate (70% cocoa solids)
375g UHT whipping cream
75g unsalted butter, cubed

Cocorico Patisserie Tarte au Citron

This is a classic that will always be on trend, but if you feel like jazzing it up, why not swap the lemon juice for grapefruit juice and add a little splash of gin!

PREPARATION TIME: 30 MINUTES, PLUS 1 HOUR MINIMUM CHILLING TIME
| BAKING TIME: 30-60 MINUTES | MAKES 12 SMALL OR 1 LARGE TARTE

METHOD

For the sweet pastry

Blend the plain flour, icing sugar and unsalted butter in a food processor until you get a sandy texture. Add the egg yolk and mix well until the all the ingredients come together.

Leave for 1 hour or overnight in the fridge. Roll out the pastry to 3-5mm thickness. Lay the rolled out dough in a tart case and gently mould it into the sides and base. Bake the pastry case in the oven at 150°c for 15 to 20 minutes. The case needs to cool before being filled.

For the lemon curd

Mix the eggs and sugar together. Mix the cornflour and lemon juice together and then combine with the egg mixture. You can either cook the curd in a microwave for about 10 minutes on full power, stopping every 1½ minutes to stir, or cook it in a bain-marie for around 45 minutes stirring periodically. Once the mixture is the right consistency, add the butter while the mixture is still hot. Cover with cling film (to prevent a skin forming) and set aside.

For the Italian meringue

Mix the caster sugar and water together and cook in a pan until the temperature of the mixture reaches 121°c. Place the egg whites in a clean electric mixer bowl with a whisk attachment. Turn the mixer on and pour the sugar syrup onto the egg whites in a steady stream. Turn the mixer up to full speed and whisk until the meringue mixture is glossy and has lots of volume. Slow the mixer down to medium speed, and then turn it off once the mixture has cooled. Transfer the meringue into a piping bag.

To assemble

Fill the tart case with the curd – both should be cooled – and then finish the tart with the meringue. Pipe in swirls or lines as desired and then scorch the top with a blowtorch to get a lovely golden brown finish.

INGREDIENTS

For the sweet pastry:
250g plain flour
125g icing sugar
125g unsalted butter, cubed
55g egg yolk

For the lemon curd:
4 eggs
300g caster sugar
40g cornflour
200ml lemon juice
225g unsalted butter, cubed

For the Italian meringue:
200g caster sugar
50ml water
100g egg white

"When you concentrate on the recipe you don't think of all the rubbish that's around. Nothing else matters."

Laurian, pâtissière, Cocorico Patisserie

CRUST AND CRUMB

The Place To Eat And Meet

Nestled in the heart of Chapel Allerton, Crust and Crumb has been serving up tasty food in a friendly and warm environment since 2010.

From a young age Nicola wanted to open a shop selling delicious food, it was just about finding the right opportunity, which happened to come along right in the middle of the recession.

CRUST AND CRUMB
110B Harrogate Road
Leeds
LS7 4NY

Telephone:
0113 2680098

Website:
www.crustand crumbbakery. co.uk

Café based in the heart of Chapel Allerton providing customers with a friendly, warm atmosphere for an enjoyable experience.

Starting out as a simple bakery, Crust and Crumb has evolved into a haven for those seeking out tasty food in a cosy setting. Each day, the counter is filled with all sorts of homemade cakes and treats, from white chocolate and raspberry brownies and salted caramel shortbread to pork and leek sausage rolls, fresh sandwiches and homemade salads. Whether you are hankering for a post yoga nibble or a hangover-curing 'full English', they have got it covered.

Having grown up on a North Yorkshire farm, Nicola has an inherent appreciation for quality local produce. This is showcased in the range of lovely ingredients used in the kitchen; their meat is from award-winning Lishman's of Ilkley and Sykes House Farm, breads and pastries come fresh from Bondgate Bakery, dressings from Yorkshire Rapeseed Oil, Ian Taylor's for eggs and Bracken Hill supply the jams and chutneys.

Working closely with Jenny, the shop manager, the team come up with a seasonal and varying menu to cater for all dietary requirements. Summer brings flatbreads and fresh salad bowls, winter is all about toasties and hearty soups – there is always something new to try. The power bar is a year-round favourite, packed with energy-giving goodness to set you up for the day. The recipe for that is a closely guarded secret so instead they've given you the secrets behind a close runner-up, the berry bakewell tart.

People from all walks of life come to socialise at Crust and Crumb while admiring the scrumptious array of food on offer, from professionals to pensioners and even dog owners; water dishes and biscuits are provided for well-behaved pooches!

Crust and Crumb is firmly part of the local community. It is the place to grab a quick takeout lunch and also the place to go for barista quality coffee, a wedge of cake and a good natter with friends. There is so much more to be found here that hasn't been mentioned so why not mosey on down and come see for yourself?

Crust and Crumb Berry Bakewell Tart

This berry bakewell tart is an all-year-round favourite at our café. It's delicious, it's wonderfully buttery and we hope you enjoy making it!

PREPARATION TIME: 15 MINUTES | BAKING TIME: 50 MINUTES | SERVES: 4

METHOD

For the pastry

Preheat the oven at 170°c and line and grease a 25cm fluted loose-bottomed flan case. Place the butter, sugar and flour in a bowl and use an electric mixer on speed 2 until the mix resembles fine breadcrumbs.

Add the egg and allow the crumb to mix to a paste. (Do not overmix at this stage) Remove from the mixer and shape the pastry into a ball then leave on the side for 5 minutes.

For the filling

Combine the ground almonds, caster sugar, butter and eggs together with an electric mixture until light and creamy. Add a dusting of flour to a flat surface and roll out the pastry with a rolling pin to approximately 5mm thickness. Carefully place this over your tin and press into the corners making sure all edges are pressed into the tin. Remove the excess pastry from the top of the tin using a palette knife.

Evenly spread the jam into the base of the tin on top of the pastry using the back of a spoon. Pour the almond filling into the tin and use a spoon to level up the sides. Evenly place the raspberries and strawberries across the tart in the almond filling, leaving the fruit still visible. Then sprinkle the flaked almonds on top for decoration.

Place in the oven for 50 minutes, after 20 minutes turn the tart around and reduce the oven temperature down to 160°c, baking for a further 30 minutes. The tart should be golden and slightly firm to touch.

Leave to cool down slightly and serve warm with a dollop of fresh cream or a scoop of indulgent ice cream.

INGREDIENTS

For the pastry:

150g unsalted butter, diced at room temperature
75g caster sugar
250g plain flour
1 free-range egg

For the filling:

250g ground almonds
250g caster sugar
250g unsalted butter, diced at room temperature
3 free-range eggs
150g strawberry jam

For the topping:

110g fresh raspberries/ strawberries
30g flaked almonds

CUTHBERT'S BAKEHOUSE

Recipe For Success

A sprinkling of love, a dash of generosity...it's time to step into Cuthbert's Bakehouse, a complete cornucopia of creativity.

CUTHBERT'S BAKEHOUSE
103 Mt Pleasant
Liverpool
L3 5TB

Telephone:
0151 709 9912

Website:
www.cuthberts
bakehouse.co.uk

Cosy wood-
furnished tea shop
with tiled floors
and industrial-
style orangery,
for cakes,
afternoon tea and
homemade hot or
light lunches.

Founders Matthew and Elaine Price developed Cuthbert's Bakehouse with the help of a scrapbook they compiled together through their love of travel and great food. They initially set up at their home back in 2006 and as the cakes continued to bake and orders continued to rise, their family home soon became a 24 hour bakehouse and it was time to expand to their very own premises.

Cuthbert's Bakehouse is now situated on one of the oldest streets in Liverpool; the building is hundreds of years old and funnily enough, it used to be a confectioner's. They even have the original oven! It became the first tea room to open in Liverpool that sells and bakes everything on-site. They now use local suppliers such as their local 'bagelry', The Liverpool Jam Company, and SourD-O for bread; this is so they can focus on making the best sweet treats and pastries.

Matt is a self-taught baker who draws a lot of his inspiration from New York; this is portrayed in their 'New Yorker' afternoon tea menu which features mini beef burgers, Reuben-style pastrami bread, cannoli, red velvet cake and New York cheesecake. Other popular choices include their salted caramel brownies, chocolate Oreo cake and their renowned velvety vanilla custard tart. Matt plans on taking this recipe to his grave!

A lot of thought and care has gone into the décor of the little bakery, from their daily specials inscribed on a huge scroll of parchment paper to their magnificent display of vintage china; Elaine's dad builds the tiered afternoon tea stands himself! They made The Independent's Top 25 Independent Afternoon Teas in 2018 and the lucky couple were also chosen to appear on television show Heston's Great British Food after researchers wanted to feature people who lived and breathed afternoon tea.

The bakery has recently expanded with an indoor garden space, which has a more industrial and open feel for diners yet compliments the traditional bakery. It has enabled the bakehouse to expand its product offering to include more vegan and dairy-free recipes as well as a hot food menu. Elaine will continue being the idea generator, and Matthew's baking skills will be responsible for bringing them to life; the duo complement each other wonderfully which is a foolproof recipe for Cuthbert's continued success.

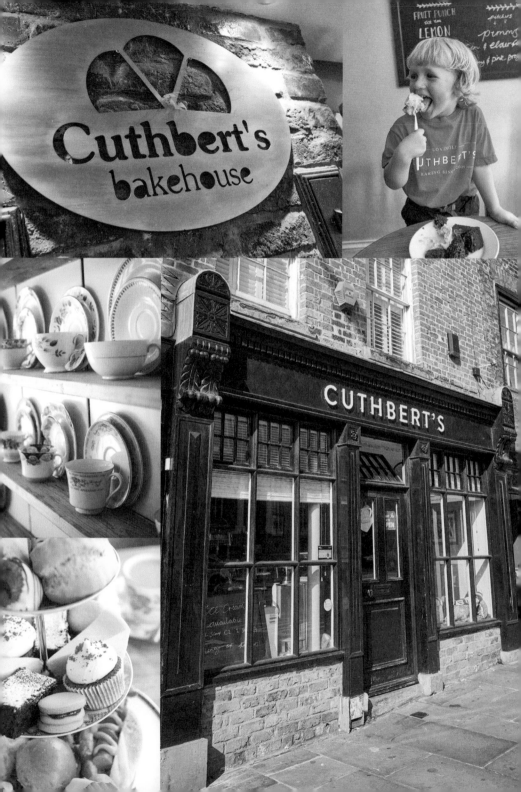

Cuthbert's Lime & Pistachio Drizzle

The secret here is the hot, sticky syrup poured onto the cake when it's singing straight from the oven, giving it a lovely moist, Madeira-like texture. It's also a great cake to experiment with flavour: pistachio and lime just aren't used enough together!

PREPARATION TIME: 20 MINUTES | BAKING TIME: 50 MINUTES | SERVES: 10-12

METHOD

Preheat the oven to 160°c then grease and line a 20cm round spring-form cake tin.

Beat the butter, sugar, lime zest and ground pistachios until pale and fluffy. If you are using an electric mixer, walk away for a while. The longer you leave it, the lighter the mixture and more voluminous the cake will be.

Turn off the mixer and carefully add the eggs, flour and baking power. Make sure the mix is properly combined before transferring into the cake tin. Place the cake into the preheated oven and bake for 50 to 55 minutes. My mam's tip for checking if a cake is ready is to listen and check 'if it's singing'. This little tip has saved me from many sunken cakes and soggy bottoms. If you can't hear the cake bubbling, pop it back in the oven for a few extra minutes.

To make the drizzle, tip the caster sugar and lime juice into a saucepan and bring to a simmer. If the limes aren't very juicy, you can add a touch of water. Once simmering, remove from the heat and place aside. Reheat once the cake is ready as it's important that the drizzle is hot.

Once the cake is ready, transfer onto a wire rack, spring open and remove the tin. Reheat the drizzle and gently pour over the warm cake before leaving to cool completely.

To finish, mix the tablespoon of lime juice and the water into the fondant icing sugar. The trick is to make sure it remains pourable, but not runny. Gently pour over the cooled cake, allowing it to drop over the sides. Finish off with a sprinkling of pistachios and enjoy as a great afternoon treat.

INGREDIENTS

For the cake:
300g softened butter
300g white caster sugar
3 limes, zested
100g pistachios, blitzed in a food processor (keep a few aside to garnish!)
6 eggs
250g self-raising flour
1 tsp baking powder

For the drizzle:
50g white caster sugar
3 limes, juiced (save a spoonful for the icing!)

For the icing:
1 tbsp lime juice
4 tbsp water
300g fondant icing sugar

DEBBIE BRYAN

Cakes And Crafternoons

Debbie Bryan is a unique blend of creative experiences, beautiful handmade gifts and delicious food and drink, located in Nottingham's historic Lace Market amongst Georgian and Victorian buildings and the city's award-winning Creative Quarter.

DEBBIE BRYAN
18 St Mary's Gate
The Lace Market
Nottingham
NG1 1PF

Telephone:
0115 9507776

Website:
www.debbie
bryan.co.uk

A unique Nottingham venture offering crafting opportunities and events that celebrate the city's heritage alongside a welcoming tea room and gift shop full of beautiful handmade products.

The eponymous owner and founder of Debbie Bryan established her textile design studio in 2007 as a designer-maker, selling national and internationally. This evolving business keeps their offer fresh and interesting, responding to customers' feedback and ensuring the company grows year on year. In 2009, this meant expanding the design studio to include a specialist retail space selling home textiles, handcrafted gifts, jewellery, ceramics, glassware and heritage pieces alongside the development of 'Crafternoons'. These can take the form of private bookable events and vastly popular scheduled creative classes.

Fast-forward to 2014 and Debbie Bryan introduced teas and freshly baked cakes, seasonal lunches and their signature afternoon tea menu, made by Hannah and Freya, who alongside Millie, Katie, and Debbie herself, comprise a welcoming and creative team. Debbie Bryan also hosts successful pop-up events, collaborating with chefs Craig Floate, Tom and Wendy Pearce of Little Ramen Shop for exceptional and diverse supper clubs, heritage tour guide Lucy Brouwer of Watson Fothergill Walk and Anne Holloway of Nottingham-based independent publisher Big White Shed.

The highly-celebrated venue is a firm favourite for those looking for a great space and excellent service to host their own parties and events: perfect for those who want to try something a little different to the norm. The combination of a creative experience, friendly service, tasty food and drink, unique gifts to purchase and the welcoming atmosphere at Debbie Bryan makes every visit special, and customers often remark that it's the perfect spot to relax and escape from the city centre hustle and bustle.

The shop and tea room is housed in a Georgian building, the interior is beautifully styled with lace heritage and textile nostalgia and is paired with an original music playlist. Debbie Bryan has cultivated a real connection with the region, not just through Nottingham's textile heritage and collections made in house, but with local suppliers who provide the tea room with fantastic local produce. Locally made real ales developed with Magpie Brewery go down nicely alongside pies and casseroles, freshly made soups and savoury scones all made in house. Freshly baked vegan and gluten-free sweet treats are also a welcome fixture of the admired tea room menu.

Nottingham Creative Business Awards: Craft Winner, Nottinghamshire Stars Awards: Best New Venture, Nottingham Independent Business of the Year and Highly Commended in Food, Drink & Things To Do are among the accolades Debbie Bryan has earned, highlighting the diversity of the venture and the love that goes into it.

Debbie Bryan
Vegan
Cream Tea

This recipe was developed in collaboration with Debbie's mother-in-law Brenda Everett, originating from her own notes made when running their family bakery business. It wasn't a vegan recipe to begin with, but after much trial and error this recipe emerged and provides a delicious alternative to a traditional cream tea or a fantastic base to add sweet or savoury flavourings to – see our recommendations in the method below.

PREPARATION TIME: 20 MINUTES | BAKING TIME: APPROX. 10 MINUTES | SERVES: 12

METHOD

Preheat the oven to 220°c and grease a baking tray with vegan butter. Add the flour, baking powder, salt and caster sugar into a mixing bowl and stir. Chop the vegan butter into small chunks and rub into dry ingredients using your fingertips.

These are our recommendations for sweet scones – choose your favourite, add to taste and mix well: glacé cherry and desiccated coconut (wash and dry cherries before adding); sultana; date and walnut (finely chopped).

This recipe also works brilliantly for savoury and non-vegan scones. Our recommendations are: pesto and fresh basil with fresh basil dressing; sun-dried tomato and sesame seed with sesame seed dressing; Stilton and walnut; feta and roasted red pepper; stem ginger and honey.

INGREDIENTS

For the scones:
450g self-raising flour
2 level tsp baking powder
Pinch of salt
85g caster sugar
170g vegan butter
200ml unsweetened almond milk

For the cream:
500ml coconut cream, chilled overnight
6 heaped tbsp icing sugar
Lemon juice, to taste

When any flavourings have been incorporated, add the unsweetened almond milk a little at a time and mix until you have soft pliable dough. Tip the scone dough onto a floured surface and knead very lightly, then roll out the dough to just over a centimetre thickness. Cut rounds from the dough and place them on the greased baking tray.

Brush the tops of all the scones with the remaining unsweetened almond milk, and bake in the preheated oven for 10 to 12 minutes until risen and golden brown. Allow to cool on the baking tray. While the scones are baking, make the whipped coconut and lemon cream. Take the coconut cream out of the fridge and add it to the icing sugar and a squeeze of lemon juice (approximately 2 teaspoons, or to taste) in a large mixing bowl. Beat until soft peaks form.

To serve

For sweet scones, dust with icing sugar and team with your favourite preserve. Serve with fresh strawberries on the side and a pot of tea to hand.

DISH AND SPOON

Dishing Up Delicious

Already well known for their delectable sweet treats, Dish and Spoon has now added a selection of savoury tastes to its menu.

Since she bought the charming little West Didsbury café And the Dish Ran Away with the Spoon, Dutch-born Annemiek has taken the thriving little eatery from strength to strength. She spent the first few years building on its reputation, serving the finest teas and coffees and the very best homemade cakes. Putting quality at the heart of the business saw Dish and Spoon, as it is now known, feature in The Independent's top 50 tea rooms in the UK.

Annemiek's sister Marloes recently joined the business, and the sisters turned their attention to adding some savoury options to the small and simple menu. The stars of the show are perhaps the beautiful open sandwiches on sourdough bread, featuring toppings like walnut and smoked red pepper with crumbled feta and rocket; hummus, spinach and sunblushed tomatoes; or serrano ham, Parmesan, rocket and basil pesto.

The theme continues with their famous cream teas; a savoury option now joins the classic cream tea on their menu. The classic cream team stars two fluffy scones with clotted cream and homemade jam, while the savoury cream tea comprises two mature cheddar and chive scones, served with cheese and homemade chutney.

Dish and Spoon is perhaps best known for its afternoon tea. Tiered cake stands are piled high with scones, finger sandwiches, savoury pastries and cakes. What makes them so special, apart from being all homemade, is that customers are able to choose not only their favourite sandwich filling but also two cakes of their choice from the irresistible cake counter. This allows each person to create their own personal afternoon tea of choice.

Annemiek's American-style brownies, one of her most popular bakes, are also available to order around the UK through her second company The Brownie Post (www.thebrowniepost.co.uk). Lovingly made and lovingly packed, they are an ideal gift for those chocoholic friends. As well as The Brownie Post, outside of the café walls, Annemiek, Marloes and their team also cater for weddings and parties, with show-stopping cakes and bespoke dessert tables for any occasion.

DISH AND SPOON
230 Burton Road,
West Didsbury
Manchester
M20 2LW

Telephone:
0161 637 5517

Website:
www.dishand
spoonfood.co.uk

Manchester café and bakery specialising in wedding cakes, dessert tables, celebration cakes and afternoon tea.

Dish and Spoon Strawberry Eton Mess Cake

Our twist on the classic English dessert, this recipe makes 12 lovely big wedges. You could cut it into smaller portions, if you prefer, but that's the way we like to serve it in the café! Scrumptious.

PREPARATION TIME: 30 MINUTES | BAKING TIME: APPROX. 1 HOUR 30 MINUTES | SERVES: 12

INGREDIENTS

For the cake:
375g plain flour
1 tsp salt
1 tbsp baking powder
125ml sour cream
125ml buttermilk
2 tsp vanilla extract
225g unsalted butter, at room temperature
450g caster sugar
4 medium eggs

For the icing:
250g mascarpone cheese
60g icing sugar
250ml double cream
1½ tsp vanilla extract

For the meringue and decoration:
2 medium egg whites
110g white caster sugar
Good-quality strawberry jam or conserve (we love Wild and Fruitful, Cumbria)
A handful of strawberries
Fresh mint leaves

METHOD

For the cake

Preheat the oven to 180°c. Grease and line the bases and sides of two deep, round, 20cm loose-bottomed cake tins with baking parchment.

In a small bowl mix the flour, salt and baking powder with a whisk. Mix the sour cream, buttermilk and vanilla in a small jug. Beat the butter and sugar with an electric handheld whisk for a few minutes until light and fluffy. Add the eggs one at a time and beat until fully incorporated. Using an electric mixer on a low speed, add the dry ingredients and buttermilk mixture to the butter, sugar and eggs in small amounts, alternating between the two. Use a spatula to scrape the mixture from the sides of the bowl and mix until no more flour is visible.

Divide the mixture between the two cake tins. Smooth and flatten without pushing it right to the edges of the tins. Bake in the preheated oven for 30 to 40 minutes, checking after 20 minutes in case it needs a foil hat to stop it from browning too much. The cakes are done when a cocktail stick comes out clean. Reduce the oven temperature to 100°c and let the cakes cool a little in the tins before taking them out and putting them onto a wire rack to cool completely.

For the icing

Whisk the mascarpone and icing sugar together until smooth. Add the double cream and continue to whisk until stiff peaks form. Gently fold in the vanilla.

For the meringue

Beat the egg whites on a low speed at first and then on high. Once they form stiff peaks start adding the sugar one spoonful at a time. Once it's been incorporated, continue to mix until glossy and stiff. Spoon the meringue mixture into a piping bag and squeeze little dollops onto a baking tray lined with parchment paper. This recipe will make more than you need for the cake, but you can snack on the rest (baker's perks!). Bake at 100˚c for 45 minutes. If they are still soft, leave them in and keep checking every 10 minutes. They are ready when they lift off the parchment easily. Remove and cool on the baking tray.

To assemble, spread half the icing onto one of the cakes. Drizzle a few spoonfuls of jam on top, then place the other cake layer on top. Spread the other half of the icing onto the top of the cake and again, drizzle some jam over it. Top the cake with halved strawberries, mint leaves and the meringues, some broken and some kept whole. Serve in big wedges.

Dish and Spoon
Blueberry & Pistachio Cake with Cardamom Buttercream

You will need two deep round 20cm loose-bottomed cake tins for this pretty layer cake.

PREPARATION TIME: 30 MINUTES | BAKING TIME: 30 MINUTES | SERVES: 10

INGREDIENTS

For the cake:
6 eggs
340g caster sugar
260g butter, melted
300g self-raising flour, sifted
190g ground pistachio nuts
75g blueberries

For the buttercream:
250g butter, softened
500g icing sugar
2 tbsp whole milk
½ tsp ground cardamom

For the decoration:
A handful of blueberries
A handful of pistachio nuts, chopped

METHOD

For the cake
Grease and line two deep 20cm round cake tins. Preheat the oven to 175°c. In a mixing bowl, whisk the eggs with the sugar until light and thick, about 5 minutes. Continue to whisk while you drizzle the melted butter into the mixture. Add the sifted flour and the ground pistachios, and gently mix. Stir in the blueberries. Divide the mixture evenly between the prepared cake tins and bake in the preheated oven for 25 to 30 minutes, checking it and turning it after 18 minutes if necessary. Turn out onto a wire rack to cool.

For the buttercream
Beat the butter with the icing sugar, milk and ground cardamom until light and fluffy.

To assemble
Ensure the sponges have cooled completely before icing. Place one of the sponges on a cake stand. Using a palette knife, spread buttercream generously and evenly on the first layer, then top with the other cake. Ice the sides and top of the cake with the rest of the buttercream, using your palette knife to create a vertical stripe up the side of the cake by pulling the palette knife from the bottom of the stand to the top.

To finish, decorate with blueberries and chopped pistachios around the edge of the cake.

Sweet Secrets

An artisan Italian micro-bakery in south-east London, Elvira's Secret Pantry is dedicated to making bespoke 'free-from' sweet and savoury delights – gluten-free, dairy-free, yeast-free – as well as offering tasty vegan options.

ELVIRA'S SECRET PANTRY
71 Groveland Road
Beckenham
BR3 3PX

Telephone:
07817 798650

Website:
www.elvirassecret
pantry.com

London-based artisan Italian micro-bakery specialising in freshly baked products, including vegan options and those free from gluten, dairy and yeast.

What do you do when you love baking but are intolerant to gluten and dairy? It can be difficult to find truly delicious baked treats that are free-from both of these common allergens. This was the dilemma that set Elvira on the course to starting up her flourishing business five years ago... and it is safe to say she has not had time to look back.

Elvira was working in art galleries while launching Elvira's Secret Pantry. She found baking to be the ideal escape from the day-to-day stresses of her busy job, and was always trying out new gluten-, dairy- and yeast-free recipes in her spare time. The first step towards transforming her passion into a business was a council-run course, where she learnt the ins and outs of setting up a market business in London. Elvira's Secret Pantry began life as a market stall at Deptford market and, over the next few months and years, the business grew organically. Other markets followed, and she became a popular trader at Crystal Palace and Beckenham markets, amongst others around south-east London.

Her Italian bakery specialises in family recipes with a creative twist, and her individuality soon led to her receiving wholesale orders from coffee shops, restaurants and independent retailers who loved her bespoke approach that enabled her to accommodate each customer. "I do everything myself," she explains, "so I can tailor any bake to very specific needs."

As well as fulfilling many wholesale orders, Elvira also sells her products online. She puts the popularity of her fare down to her simple approach of using seasonal, organic and additive-free ingredients. "I only bake things that I love," Elvira admits, which means that her passion for flavour comes across in every bite.

The latest addition to Elvira's Secret Pantry comes in the form of her baking classes. These can take place in her kitchen or in customers' own homes. Whatever she is teaching people – how to make one of her favourite cakes, tarts or vegan cookies – the classes always have an informal and friendly atmosphere.

With her wholesale orders continually increasing, demand for personal orders popping through on her website and a plethora of classes in the diary, it looks like Elvira's Secret Pantry might not be so secret in south-east London any more.

Elvira's Secret Pantry
Orange, Coconut and Rosemary Cake

Who says you need flour to make a delicious cake? Elvira's flourless cake is full of zingy flavour, punctuated with a subtle earthy taste from the rosemary.

PREPARATION TIME: 40 MINUTES | BAKING TIME: 50 MINUTES | SERVES: 8

METHOD

For the cake

Preheat the oven to 180°c /160°c fan. Grease and line an 20cm round, loose-bottomed cake tin. Beat the dairy-free spread, sugar and orange zest in a large bowl until light and creamy. In a separate bowl, combine the almond, coconut, polenta, baking powder and finely chopped rosemary; beat some of this into the butter-sugar mixture, followed by 1 egg, then alternate dry ingredients and eggs, beating all the while. Pour the mixture into the tin and bake for 40 to 50 minutes, or until the surface is golden-brown and a skewer inserted into the middle comes out clean. Remove the tin from the oven, leave to cool for 15 minutes.

For the syrup

In a small saucepan, warm the orange juice, blossom water, honey and water. Prick the cake quite densely with a toothpick, and then generously pour over the syrup. Leave it to cool for a further 20 minutes. Gently remove the cake from the tin and transfer to a wire rack to cool completely.

For the decoration

Whisk together the icing sugar, dairy-free spread and nut oil until smooth. Spread the icing over the cake and sprinkle with coconut flakes.

Photography: Stuart Matthews

INGREDIENTS

For the cake:

200g dairy-free spread
180g unrefined golden caster sugar
1 organic orange, zested
100g ground almond
80g desiccated coconut
100g polenta
½ tbsp baking powder
3 fresh rosemary leaves
3 medium organic eggs

For the syrup:

1 organic orange, juiced
1 tbsp orange blossom water
1 tbsp honey
2 tbsp water

For the icing and decoration:

30g icing sugar, sifted
20g dairy-free spread
1 tbsp walnut oil
Coconut flakes, for decoration

"I only bake things that I love myself."

Elvira, founder, Elvira's Secret Pantry

HODMEDOD

Spilling The Beans

Champion of home-grown pulses and grains, Hodmedod is reintroducing us to traditional British staple foods and developing the production of new crops, and they have some fabulously original ideas for what to do with them.

HODMEDOD LTD
The Bean Store
Unit 1
The Studios
Brampton
Halesworth
Suffolk NR34 8DQ

Telephone:
01986 467567

Website:
www.hodmedods.
co.uk

Hodmedod works with British farmers to source and provide British-grown beans, peas and quinoa.

Nick Saltmarsh, Josiah Meldrum and William Hudson founded Hodmedod in 2012 in order to bring home-grown fava beans (small seeded dried broad beans) back to British kitchens. These tasty and nutritious pulses have been grown in Britain since the Iron Age and were once an important part of our diet. British chefs and home cooks alike are discovering they can be an excellent substitute for chickpeas in falafel and hummus, make delicious thick and creamy soups, lovely dal and curries, and the split beans don't even need soaking before cooking.

Nick, Josiah and William are also continually on the lookout for other less well-known foods that can be grown on British farms. Among Hodmedod's most popular products are 'Black Badger' carlin peas and quinoa from the plains of Essex. In 2017 they harvested the first ever British commercial crop of lentils and now sell British-grown chia, smoked quinoa and emmer, a delicious and nutritious ancestor of our modern wheat.

The business has grown as more people are becoming interested in adopting a more sustainable diet. Vegetarianism and veganism are at an all-time high but the biggest growth is in the number of people trying to reduce the amount of meat in their diets. Eating more pulses and grains is the ideal way to achieve this while maintaining a healthy diet. Hodmedod's efforts to produce more delicious and sustainable sources of vegetable protein were recognised in 2017 when they were awarded 'Best Food Producer' in the BBC Food and Farming Awards.

As well as the dried products, Hodmedod also offers a range of canned pulses and roasted beans and peas. The aim is to have us all filling our cupboards with these versatile, protein-packed products, celebrating forgotten British food heroes and discovering new British crops for a more sustainable future.

So what is a hodmedod anyway? Debate around this old East Anglian dialect word rages between Suffolk and Norfolk; depending on who you're talking to it might be a hedgehog, snail, ammonite or even a curl of hair. What these meanings have in common is that they're all small and round, just like the ancient beans, peas and grains Hodmedod is bringing back to our kitchens.

Hodmedod
Carlin Pea & Ginger Gluten-free Chocolate Cake

The ginger and chocolate combine with the peas to make a moist, rich cake which is not overly sweet and looks just as good as it tastes.

PREPARATION TIME: 45-50 MINUTES | BAKING TIME: 45-50 MINUTES | SERVES: 12

INGREDIENTS
For the cake:
175g unsalted butter, plus extra for greasing
Cocoa powder, for dusting
200g good-quality dark chocolate or chocolate chips
3 tbsp syrup from the jar of stem ginger
200g cooked Hodmedod's Carlin Peas (or canned Hodmedod's Carlin Peas are an excellent alternative if you don't have time to soak and cook dry peas)
200g light muscovado sugar
1½ tsp ground ginger
4 eggs, separated
4 pieces (about 80g) of stem ginger, chopped

For the decoration:
125g good-quality dark chocolate
80ml double cream
20g unsalted butter
2 tbsp of syrup from the jar of stem ginger
1-2 pieces of stem ginger, chopped

METHOD

Grease a 23cm spring-release cake tin with butter and line the bottom with baking paper. Dust the sides with cocoa powder. Preheat the oven to 185°c. Break up the chocolate and put it in a heatproof bowl with the butter and ginger syrup. Put the bowl over a saucepan of gently simmering water and stir occasionally until melted. Do not let the bottom of the bowl come into contact with the simmering water. Put the peas into a food processor and process until resembling coarse ground almonds. Add the sugar, ground ginger and egg yolks to the pea mix and process again until combined. Turn the mixture out into a large bowl and stir in the chopped ginger.

In a separate clean bowl, whisk the four egg whites until stiff. Stir the melted chocolate, butter and ginger syrup into the pea, ginger, egg yolk and sugar mix. Using a metal spoon, gently fold half the egg whites into the chocolate mixture, then fold in the remaining half, incorporating as much air in the mixture as possible. Pour the mixture into the prepared cake tin and bake in the preheated oven for 45 to 50 minutes until set. Don't worry if the cake cracks slightly. Remove from the oven and leave to cool on a wire rack for 10 minutes before taking off the outer ring.

When the cake is completely cool, make the chocolate covering. Put the chocolate, cream, butter and ginger syrup in a heatproof bowl set over gently simmering water and stir until melted, smooth and glossy. Do not let the bottom of the bowl come into contact with the simmering water.

Spoon the chocolate over the top of the cake and spread to the edges with a palette knife. Leave to set a little before distributing the remaining pieces of ginger on the top. When cutting the cake, wipe the knife blade between cuts to ensure a beautifully clean cut.

HOMEMADE BY THELMA'S

From Brunch To Bistro Nights

Set in the leafy suburb of Nether Edge, Homemade by Thelma's has settled into a new home and has added weekly bistro nights to its list of charms...

HOMEMADE BY THELMA'S
2-4 Nether Edge Road
Sheffield S7 1RU

Telephone:
07774 013438

Website:
www.homemade-sheffield.co.uk

A café and bistro that prides itself on fresh, seasonal, home-cooked food: sandwiches, salads and cakes by day, and restaurant-style bistro nights on Friday evenings.

From their new premises in Nether Edge, Emily and Becky are welcoming lots of exciting new changes to one of Sheffield's favourite little cafés. Homemade by Thelma's started life back in 2011 when Emily Rowley and her sister May decided to open a café in the thriving foodie area of Sharrow Vale Road.

A love of good food ran in the Rowley blood, and the sisters named the café after their grandma who was a great lover of eating! The café was a huge success with its lovely selection of breakfast, lunch and cakey offerings, and the business soon outgrew its first home. In 2013 they moved to larger premises in Nether Edge, which gave them chance to try their hand at formal cooking for a weekly bistro night. On Friday nights the café becomes a gorgeous bistro, where guests bring their own drinks and enjoy some top-quality food in a relaxed environment.

The bistro night menu changes every month – the team are big fans of seasonal cooking, so the menu will often reflect what is available locally and seasonally. Vegetarians, meat-eaters, vegans and those avoiding gluten are all well catered for – the ethos is very much that everyone should be able to enjoy great food.

After four years of hard work building the business to what it is today, May decided it was time to hang up her apron and move on to something new. In November 2015 Becky Furber (who had been their right hand woman for the previous year, and Emily's best friend!) stepped up and became joint owner with Emily. The pair love working together and are known for being pretty much inseparable – despite spending six days a week together at work, they're together most evenings and even go on holiday together!

Becky and Emily pay tribute to their small but amazing team of staff: "They show us an amazing amount of love, dedication and hard work and we really are like a strange little family!"

No two days are the same at Homemade by Thelma's. Each day they offer five beautiful salads to accompany the specials and a range of deli-style sandwiches, bagels and quesadillas. They are always testing out new recipes, particularly gluten-free ones, "so that everyone can have a slice of cake!"

They have also now launched their All You Can Eat Brunch Club on the first Sunday of each month - so for those of you who simply can't get enough of Thelma's, now you don't have to!

Homemade by Thelma's
Apricot, Rose and Pistachio Polenta Cake

This gluten-free cake is a favourite at Homemade by Thelma's – it's as pretty as it is tasty!

PREPARATION TIME: 15 MINUTES | BAKING TIME: 40 MINUTES | SERVES: 9

METHOD
For the cake
Preheat the oven to 170°c. Grease and line a 30cm spring-form cake tin.

Whisk together the butter and sugar. Add the eggs and whisk until well combined. Add the ground almonds and polenta and stir in with a wooden spoon. Stir in the rose water, pistachios and apricots and transfer to the prepared tin. Bake in the preheated oven for about 40 minutes, checking after 30 minutes. Remove from the oven and allow to cool completely before decorating.

To decorate
Make a thick icing using the icing sugar and water and drizzle it in zig-zags across the cake. Scatter with pistachios, apricots and rose petals.

INGREDIENTS
For the cake:
375g butter
375g caster sugar
4 large eggs
300g ground almonds
100g fine polenta
Splash of rose water
75g pistachios, finely chopped
75g dried apricots, roughly chopped

To decorate:
Icing sugar
Water
Pistachios and dried apricots, finely chopped
Rose petals

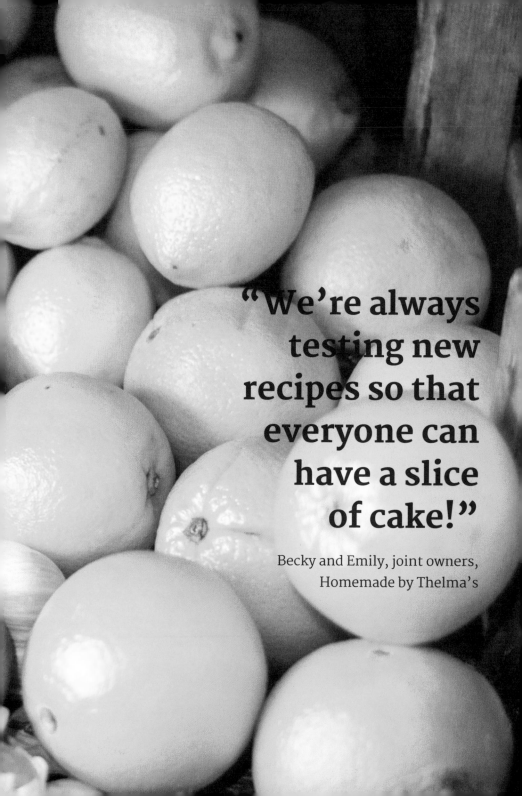

"We're always testing new recipes so that everyone can have a slice of cake!"

Becky and Emily, joint owners, Homemade by Thelma's

HOMEMADE

From The Heart And The home

Brunch, lunch, cakes and a place to feel welcome: Homemade café is bursting with homemade goods, locally sourced and made with real love.

Homemade is a venture that has grown organically from a simple ethos that revolves around cooking proper, honest food for people to enjoy. Jasmin founded Homemade in 2005, when the first café was established in Hockley. She wanted to create a space that could look and feel something like an extension of her own dining room, having regularly cooked for groups of friends around her house, with that same sociable atmosphere that centred on good food, made well.

Homemade at the Forest Recreation Ground Pavilion opened in 2014 after a series of successful pop-ups, and now after closing the city centre premises, the whole Homemade operation is at the Forest Rec. The move was motivated by shifting the focus more onto the baking, developing trade in wholesale and special occasion cakes. Baking HQ is in the other building on the park, a grade II listed lodge gate house, built in 1857, which resembles a Greek revival temple. In there the delicious treats are created and the front room has been turned into a cute coffee kiosk for passers by to admire a piece of Nottingham's history, with a coffee or fresh pastry in hand.

Jasmin refers to the Forest Rec as an oasis, so close to the centre of Nottingham yet incredibly peaceful. Homemade welcomes walkers from the park, including those accompanied by muddy paws and little ones! It serves a brunch and lunch menu, with just as many delicious cakes and hot drinks, alongside ice cream for summer days. The menu changes according to the season and Jasmin's creative flair is evident in the café interiors with their quirky antique decorations and vintage touches.

Having won awards both locally and nationally, Homemade is the place to go, not just for a relaxing and tasty spot of indulgence, but for special occasion catering and spectacular cakes made to order. Sticking with simplicity and bringing people food from the heart has made Jasmin's venture a popular name in the city, proving that when it's Homemade, it just tastes better!

HOMEMADE PAVILION, FOREST REC.
Forest Recreation Ground Pavilion
Mansfield Road
Nottingham
NG5 2BU

Telephone:
0115 978 1608

Website:
www.homemadecafe.com

A beautiful location with a unique atmosphere serving locally sourced, homemade goodness, with catering options for events and cakes to order.

The Lodge

Sticky Toffee & Ginger Cake ♡

Carrot Cake ♡

Raspberry & Lemon

Homemade Jasmin's Peanut Butter, Banana & Chocolate Chip Cake

The combination of peanut butter, banana and chocolate is gloriously decadent and creates a lovely moist cake. It's important to use ripe bananas – even ones that have gone brown – as they will be sweeter and easier to mash.

PREPARATION TIME: 30 MINUTES | BAKING TIME: APPROX. 35 MINUTES | SERVES: 10

INGREDIENTS

For the cake:
250g salted butter, softened (you can use unsalted instead, but you'll need to add a pinch of salt)
250g soft brown sugar
4 eggs
1 tbsp vanilla extract
300g self-raising flour
250g crunchy peanut butter
2 ripe bananas, mashed
150g dark chocolate chips

For the buttercream:
150g softened butter
200g icing sugar
70g crunchy peanut butter
50g best quality dark cocoa
100g dark chocolate, melted
100g dry roasted peanuts

METHOD

For the cake

Preheat the oven to 170°c and line two 23cm sandwich cake tins.

Using an electric hand whisk, whip up the butter to a smooth, rich looking consistency. Then slowly whisk in the soft brown sugar. Whisk the eggs and vanilla extract together in a separate bowl. Using a sieve, add half the flour, followed by half the egg mixture. Mix with the hand whisk then do the same again with the remaining flour, adding in the rest of the egg mixture until smooth.

Add the peanut butter and the mashed bananas and whisk into the mixture. Fold in the chocolate chips then distribute the cake mixture evenly between the two prepared baking tins, spreading it out with a palette knife or the back of a spoon as necessary. Place in the oven to bake for approximately 35 minutes. Once done, remove the cakes from the oven and leave them in the tins to cool down for a good hour before icing.

For the buttercream

Whisk the butter, then sift in the icing sugar using a sieve and whisk to a smooth consistency. Add the peanut butter, cocoa and melted chocolate and whisk everything together. Use the buttercream as the sandwich filling for the cake and spread a good layer on the top as well. Once the cake is iced, sprinkle the top of the cake with dry roasted peanuts for decoration.

Homemade Jasmin's Toffee Apple Cake

If using unsalted butter, add a pinch of salt to the cake mixture. The crushed pecans are easily made by wrapping whole pecans in a cloth or sealable bag, and bashing them with a rolling pin. The weight of the apples is taken after peeling and coring.

PREPARATION TIME: 30 MINUTES | BAKING TIME: APPROX. 35 MINUTES | SERVES: 12

INGREDIENTS

For the cake:
250g apples, peeled and cored
1 tbsp ground cinnamon
1 tbsp ground mixed spice
250g salted butter, softened
250g soft dark brown sugar
4 eggs
1 tbsp vanilla extract
300g self-raising flour

For the buttercream:
150g soft butter
50ml stem ginger syrup
½ tsp ground ginger
200g icing sugar

For the toffee drizzle:
150g caster sugar
40g butter
100ml double cream

For the topping:
2 apples, thinly sliced
1 lemon, juiced
80g pecans, crushed

METHOD

For the cake
Preheat the oven to 170°c then line two 23cm sandwich cake tins with baking parchment. Place the apples in a saucepan with about 100ml of water over a low heat until softened, then stir in the cinnamon and mixed spice. Set aside.

Using an electric handheld whisk or Kitchen Aid, whip up the butter to a nice smooth consistency, then slowly whisk in the brown sugar. Whisk the eggs and vanilla extract together. Using a sieve, add half of the flour, followed by half of the egg mixture, and mix thoroughly. Do the same again with the remaining flour and egg mixture until smooth. Fold the cooked spiced apple into the mixture. Distribute the cake batter evenly between the two sandwich tins; you may need to spread it out with a palette knife or the back of a spoon. Then place in the oven to bake for approximately 35 minutes. Keep an eye on the cakes as times may vary depending on your oven. Once cooked, remove from the oven, leaving the cakes in the tins to cool down for a good hour before icing.

For the buttercream icing
Whisk the butter until smooth and lighter in colour, then whisk in the stem ginger syrup and ground ginger. Using a sieve, gradually add the icing sugar and whisk to a smooth consistency.

For the toffee drizzle
This can be made ahead of time and stored in a sealable container. In a non-stick saucepan, melt the sugar slowly over a gentle heat. Do not stir! Once the sugar starts to bubble, add the butter and melt through, then stir in the double cream, and set aside to cool and thicken. Baker's tip: if your toffee cools too much, it can be gently reheated for 20 seconds in the microwave in a plastic tub.

To assemble
Top the first cake with a generous layer of the ginger buttercream, then sandwich the second cake on top of that, and cover in a thin layer of the buttercream. Top with slices of apple, brushed with lemon juice to stop them browning. Arrange in a fan. Drizzle the cake with toffee, creating a drip effect down the sides. Finish off the cake with some smashed pecans in the centre of the cake, then cut into generous slices and enjoy!

JERVAULX ABBEY TEAROOMS

A Labour Of Love

By focusing on delicious home baking and cooking – a shared love in the family-run venture – the Burdons have brought people to the magnificent Jervaulx Abbey through their successful tearoom.

JERVAULX ABBEY TEAROOMS
Jervaulx
Ripon
North Yorkshire
HG4 4PH

Telephone:
01677 460 391

Website:
www.
jervaulxabbey.
com/tearooms

Family-run tearoom in rural North Yorkshire on the site of a privately owned abbey.

The Burdon family – Ian, Carol, Gayle and Anna – have been welcoming visitors to the Jervaulx Abbey Tearoom in North Yorkshire since it opened in 1994. They have also had the huge responsibility of preserving the atmospheric abbey ruins, through hard work and lots of delicious home baking and cooking in the family-run tearoom. Jervaulx is one of the largest privately owned Cistercian abbeys in the UK maintained solely by its owners, and has been in the family since Ian's father bought the land and what remained of the twelfth century abbey in 1971.

In 1993, Ian and his wife Carol repurchased part of the estate and converted a couple of greenhouses into the Jervaulx Abbey Tearoom. Their daughters Gayle and Anna returned home to help develop the business further, and together they are now dedicated to managing the remaining monastic buildings that make up the beautiful abbey ruins. The tearoom's reputation grew steadily right from the start, and its popularity was evidenced by an extension in 2014, which was planned as a private events venue, but actually ended up in use almost daily to accommodate all the customers! The extension is now a cake studio for Gayle, who won a national award in 2019 for her celebration and wedding cake business, Where The Ribbon Ends.

Carol, Anna and Gayle make and sell a range of freshly made food, including lunches, sweet treats, jams, chutneys and relishes, using ingredients sourced locally from producers around Yorkshire. You could even say they've followed in the footsteps of the monks who originally lived and worked within the abbey's walls! The production of meat, fish, beer, a ewe's milk cheese now recognised as a precursor to today's famous Wensleydale variety, wool, fruit and vegetables would have been the Cistercian monks' livelihood, and essential to keep the community and their home thriving.

The Burdon family's tearoom is deeply connected to the area and of course to their abbey, something they are all very proud of. As Anna puts it, "to spend our lifetimes preserving the abbey is as great a contribution as we could ask for, and to have done part of that by indulging our love of home baking and cooking together is something very special indeed."

Jervaulx Abbey Vegan Carrot Cake

We love carrot cake here at Jervaulx. Not only is it unbelievably tasty, you can convince yourself you're eating something healthy; it does have veggies in after all!

PREPARATION TIME: 15 MINUTES, PLUS 30 MINUTES COOLING TIME
| BAKING TIME: 45 MINUTES | SERVES: 8

METHOD
Preheat the oven to 160°c or 140°c fan and line a 20cm cake tin.

Mix the plain flour, salt, baking powder, bicarbonate of soda, cinnamon, raisins and walnuts (if using) together in a large bowl. Add the carrots and oil to the dry ingredients and mix everything together using a wooden spoon. Once that's well combined, add the orange juice and sugar and stir thoroughly, making sure there are no lumps of carrot remaining. Carefully spoon the mixture into the prepared tin and bake for 45 minutes or until a skewer comes out clean.

Leave the cake to cool for 30 minutes before turning out onto a plate or cake stand.

INGREDIENTS
510g plain flour
½ tsp salt
2 tsp baking powder
½ tsp bicarbonate of soda
1 tsp cinnamon
100g raisins
100g walnuts (optional)
300g carrots, peeled and grated
140ml corn oil
115ml fresh orange juice
255g caster sugar

Jervaulx Abbey Lemony Treacle Tart

This tart is not only a real treat with a cup of tea in the afternoon, it doubles up as a pudding after Sunday lunch served warm with ice cream. It is one of our favourites to make at the tearooms, and also one of our favourites to eat too!

PREPARATION TIME: 10 MINUTES, PLUS 30 MINUTES CHILLING TIME
| BAKING TIME: 30-35 MINUTES | SERVES: 8

METHOD

For the pastry
Put the flour, salt and margarine in a large bowl and rub together until the mixture resembles breadcrumbs. Add the egg gradually while combining until you have a firm dough. If the mixture doesn't come together easily, add a tiny splash of cold water. Wrap in cling film and chill for 30 minutes. Roll out the pastry and line a 23cm loose-bottomed tart tin, trimming off any excess that overhangs the sides. Store in the fridge until needed.

For the filling
Preheat the oven to 180°c or 160°c fan. Warm the syrup in a pan, ensuring that it doesn't boil, and then stir in the breadcrumbs, lemon zest, oats and eggs. Pour into the pastry case and bake the treacle tart in the preheated oven for 30 to 35 minutes. The filling may still be slightly wobbly after this time but it will set as it cools. Leave in the tin to cool before turning out.

INGREDIENTS

For the pastry:
170g self-raising flour
Pinch of salt
85g cold margarine
1 large egg, beaten
Cold water (if needed)

For the filling:
795g golden syrup
125g breadcrumbs
1½ lemons, zested
55g rolled oats
2 large eggs, whisked

Jervaulx Abbey Rhubarb and Almond Cake

The sharpness and sweetness of the rhubarb combined with that unique almond flavour tastes incredible. With the addition of custard icing, which we love, it makes for the perfect dessert in cake form.

PREPARATION TIME: 30 MINUTES, PLUS OVERNIGHT CHILLING TIME | BAKING TIME: 1 HOUR 25 MINUTES | SERVES: 10

METHOD
Preheat the oven to 170°c or 150 °c fan and line the base of a 23cm round tin with greaseproof paper.

For the cake
Cut the rhubarb into 3 inch sections, place onto a baking tray and cover with a splash of orange juice and drizzle of honey. Bake in the oven for 8-10 minutes. Once done, allow to cool and then drain the rhubarb pieces in a sieve, keeping the juices to one side.

Cream together the margarine and sugar until light and fluffy. Beat in the eggs one at a time, adding a little flour in between to avoid splitting. Add the rest of the flour, the ground almonds and baking powder and mix well.

Pour half of the mixture into the prepared tin, and add half the rhubarb pieces in a circle following the curve of the tin. Add the remaining mixture and then top with the rest of the rhubarb pieces, pressing them in to the mixture to keep the top flat and avoid any burnt bits. Sprinkle over the flaked almonds and Demerara sugar. Bake the cake for 1 hour and 25 minutes, or until a skewer comes out clean. Leave to cool and remove from the tin.

For the custard icing
Add all of the ingredients to a mixing bowl and beat together for 5-10 minutes. Beat well to ensure the custard powder has been completely mixed and you can't taste or feel any graininess. For a creamy taste, leave in the fridge overnight. Remove from the fridge and allow the icing to warm to room temperature. Mix well again and begin to ice your cake.

To finish
For an added hit of flavour, drizzle a dash of the rhubarb cooking juice over the cake once it's baked and still hot from the oven. The juices will soak into the cake and enhance the rhubarb flavour. Slice the cake in half, spread a thick layer of the custard icing over the bottom layer and place the top part of the cake back on. Place the cake into the fridge to set the icing and then enjoy.

INGREDIENTS
For the cake:
340g rhubarb
Splash of orange juice
Drizzle of honey
285g margarine
295g caster sugar
4 eggs
170g self-raising flour
340g ground almonds
2 tsp baking powder
3 tbsp flaked almonds
Sprinkle of Demerara sugar

For the custard icing:
170g butter, at room temperature
370g icing sugar
30g custard powder
30ml milk

> **"To spend our lifetimes preserving the abbey is as great a contribution as we could ask for, and to have done part of that by indulging our love of home baking and cooking together is something very special indeed."**
>
> The Burdon family, Jervaulx Abbey Tearoom

KENYON HALL FARM

From Farm To Fork

With a farm shop, plant centre, café and pick-your-own seasonal fruits and vegetables, Kenyon Hall Farm is a family farm with lots to offer.

KENYON HALL FARM
Winwick Lane
Croft
Warrington
WA3 7ED

Telephone:
01925 765531

Website:
www.kenyonhall.co.uk

Delivery business:
www.northernharvest.co.uk

Set in the Cheshire countryside is the family-run Kenyon Hall Farm Shop, café, plant centre and 'pick-your-own' fields.

For Tod and Barbara Bulmer, Kenyon Hall Farm is not just their family business, it's their family heritage. They took over the farm in 1978, but Tod's family have been working the land here for a staggering 500 years, first as tenants until Tod's grandfather bought the farm in 1919. With such strong links to the land and the county, Tod and Barbara are passionate about keeping the Bulmer family farm as an intrinsic part of the local community.

When Barbara and Tod first took over the sleepy arable farm, they decided to plant the first two acres of strawberries and introduce the pick-your-own enterprise. Some herbs followed, from which the plant centre developed, and gradually Kenyon Hall Farm expanded into a thriving foodie destination.

Today the farm is unique in the north west as the pick-your-own has expanded to incorporate a whole host of seasonal fruits and vegetables: strawberries, raspberries and currants from June; garden peas, mangetout and broad beans from July; onions, blackberries and sweetcorn from August; right through to pumpkins and squashes in October.

In the café, Barbara always bases her menu around the fresh seasonal produce they have available. The Manchester Tart recipe overleaf is made using homemade jam from home-grown raspberries! Everything served in the café – soups, stews, sandwiches, fry ups, salads and cakes – is made fresh in the kitchen. It's a vision of proper farmhouse cooking.

The eco-friendly farm shop (a mile of pipes heat it from underground!) brings together products from a range of farmers and producers, such as organic meat, free-range eggs, seasonal fruits and veggies, artisan bread, their own award-winning jams and chutneys, and a range of ales and ciders from local breweries.

The evolution of Kenyon Hall Farm continues to this day, and there's now something interesting going on almost all year round. Seasonal attractions such as the plant centre in spring, the summer pick-your-own season, and the pumpkin festival at Halloween remain firm favourites. More recent additions such as the Easter Egg Hunt and the autumnal Maize Maze have been complemented by year-round 'Junior Farmer' events where the little ones get to try their hand at a range of farming activities. For Tod and Barbara, it's fantastic to see the future of British farming continuing to grow!

Kenyon Hall Farm
Manchester Tart

This old-fashioned dessert is a winner in our café and has been for years. Some of our customers say it reminds them of school (in a good way). We make it using our homemade raspberry jam from our very own raspberries!

PREPARATION TIME: 20 MINUTES | BAKING TIME: APPROXIMATELY 45 MINUTES | SERVES:

METHOD
Preheat the oven to 200°c.

For the pastry
Put the flour into a large mixing bowl or food processor. Add the cubed lard and margarine then rub or process the fats into the flour until the mixture resembles breadcrumbs. Add three tablespoons of cold water and bind the mixture to a soft but dry dough. Add more water if required.
Smooth the dough into a round on a clean, lightly floured surface and roll the pastry out to approximately 2cm larger than the dish. We make ours in a 22cm Pyrex flan dish. Lift the pastry with the rolling pin on to the dish then ease it into the base and up the sides with your fingers, pressing to eliminate air bubbles.
Line the pastry case with greaseproof paper and baking beans or dried peas reserved for this purpose.
Bake in the hot oven for 10 to 15 minutes until the pastry is golden brown. Remove the baking beans and paper and return the case to the oven until the base is done. Allow to cool.

For the filling
Spread the Kenyon Hall Homemade Raspberry Jam over the base of the pastry and layer the sliced bananas thinly over it.
Put the custard powder and sugar into a jug and blend to a smooth paste with little of the milk.
Boil the rest of the milk and pour in to the custard mix, stirring well. Return the custard to a clean pan and bring back to the boil, stirring gently but continually Remove from the heat, keep stirring, then pour the custard over the bananas and jam.

For the topping
Sprinkle the top with desiccated coconut; this stops a skin from forming on the custard. Decorate with glacé cherries, leave to cool then refrigerate to set the custard.

INGREDIENTS
For the pastry:
340g plain flour
85g lard, cut into small cubes
85g hard margarine, cut into small cubes

For the filling:
3 heaped tbsp Kenyon Hall Homemade Raspberry Jam
2 large bananas, sliced
55g custard powder
55g sugar
840ml milk

For the topping:
Desiccated coconut
Glacé cherries

LAVENDER BAKEHOUSE

Chalford Charm

Customers return to Lavender Bakehouse time and time again for an irresistible taste of Cotswolds hospitality, along with all those delicious homemade goodies.

Lavender Bakehouse and Coffee Shop is owned by Tina Bowden who built the business from scratch with the help of family and friends. Having worked in the food industry all her life, the overriding passion had always been to open her own business.

LAVENDER BAKEHOUSE & COFFEE SHOP
20 London Road
Chalford
Stroud
GL6 8NW

Telephone:
01453 889239

Website:
www.lavender
bakehouse.co.uk

Coffee shop bistro serving breakfast, lunch, afternoon tea, coffee and cake.

"I used to drive past the shop on my way back from London late on a Friday night and always thought it would make a brilliant coffee shop or bistro," recalls Tina. It was originally the local Co-operative store for the area with its own bakery and dairy, and retains some of its heritage alongside fresh new charm, including a lovely hand-painted mural by an artist friend.

The canal-side location in Chalford draws in all who pass by, from dog walkers and cyclists to walking groups who have come to the area to enjoy its beautiful countryside. They use local produce from small suppliers where possible, such as Godsells cheese, Day's Cottage apple juice and cider, wines from Woodchester Valley Vineyard, coffee from Coffee Roastery based in Gloucester, beer from Stroud Brewery and even a lavender marmalade from Selsley Foods. They also use award-winning, locally produced sausages and bacon in their famous breakfasts... In their first year they were voted one of the top 50 breakfast venues by The Independent.

Each day starts long before breakfast, though. At 5am the team begin baking the cakes and patisseries, which have become so renowned they are now supplied to various other businesses too, as well as being sold in the shop. The shop also does a roaring trade in outside catering, providing breakfast and lunch platters for private events and business functions, and many local independent cafés and restaurants with a full range of cakes and desserts including a range of vegan and gluten-free options.

By lunchtime it is a hive of activity with homemade soups being served, salads on the deli counter and the smell of freshly made savoury tarts wafting from the kitchen. Later on, the vintage cake stands take centre stage as the traditional afternoon teas are always made into a special event. White table linens, beautiful china and, of course, a mouth-watering selection of miniature sandwiches, savouries, pastries and cakes makes it a memorable afternoon each and every time.

Lavender Bakehouse Orange and Lavender Cake

The citrus kick of this gluten-free cake comes from both oranges and lemons; you will need two lemons and four oranges altogether, using the zest for the cake and then the juice in the glaze.

PREPARATION TIME: 15 MINUTES | BAKING TIME: 60 MINUTES | SERVES: 12

METHOD
For the cake
Grease and line a 25cm round cake tin. Preheat the oven to 160°c.

Mix together the ground almonds, sugar and baking powder. Add the oil and eggs at the same time.

Add the zest of the lemons and oranges and the dried lavender. Mix to combine and pour into the prepared tin.

Bake in the preheated oven and bake for an initial 30 minutes. If the cakes are browning too much after 30 minutes, turn the temperature down to 140°c and cover the top with foil. Keep checking the cake every 15 minutes until done.

For the glaze
Put the juice from the lemons and oranges into a heavy-based saucepan and add the sugar, cloves and cinnamon. Leave on a medium heat until the syrup has reduced by half. Pour half over the baked cake and keep the rest for decoration.

INGREDIENTS
For the cake:
700g ground almonds
600g caster sugar
6 tsp (90g) gluten-free baking powder
750ml sunflower oil
16 eggs, beaten
2 lemons, zested
4 oranges, zested
4 tsp dried lavender

For the glaze:
2 lemons, juiced
4 oranges, juiced
200g caster sugar
4 cloves
4 tsp cinnamon

"Our vintage cake stands take centre stage in the café as the traditional afternoon teas are always made into a special event here – they are a really important part of the shop for me."

Tina, owner, Lavender Bakehouse

THE MALL DELI

West Country On A Plate

A deli at the front and a café at the back, The Mall Deli in historic Clifton Village is a true foodie paradise where local produce is championed, dishes are home-cooked and regulars have been coming back for decades.

THE MALL DELI
14 The Mall
Clifton
Bristol BS8 4DR

Telephone:
0117 973 4440

Website:
www.themalldeli.
co.uk

A traditional deli and café in the heart of Clifton Village which has been serving delicious food to our customers for 30 years.

Although Kate has been running the deli and café since 2010, The Mall Deli has actually been a key part of Clifton Village for over 30 years. It's fair to say it has been through many a change over those years – at one point being linked by an archway to the butchers next door – but it has always been an important part of life for people in the Village.

The rich history of the Village (which is older than Bristol itself), the elegant architecture, the iconic attractions and the plethora of diverse independent shops creates a mix that is difficult to beat. When Kate returned to Bristol and took over the deli, she and her team wanted to cherish what had made this long-standing business so special while evolving the product range, building relationships with local independent producers and engaging with customers old and new.

The deli staff team, which has grown hugely, is perhaps what makes The Mall Deli such a success. "Our kitchen and deli teams work really hard to ensure that we have a wide variety of fresh homemade food every day, and that we keep our deli stocked up with wonderful goodies," says Kate. "And in the café, our deli assistants and baristas are on first name terms with many of our regulars. They make fantastic coffees and teas (using locally roasted Extract coffee beans and tea from The Bristol Tea Company) and serve generous slices of our homemade cakes from behind a tiny coffee station!"

The welcoming interior is always busy with a real mix of people; its rustic feel and unpretentious ambience is testament to the team's effort to make The Mall Deli a place where the whole community can feel at home. The deli at the front is an Aladdin's cave of goodies, shelves heaving with locally sourced products and fridges packed with homemade dishes.

With The Mall Deli always on the hunt for new local produce, it is set to remain a little foodie haven in the heart of Clifton for many more years to come.

The Mall Deli Chocolate Stout Cake

Inspired by recipes we've tried out for chocolate Guinness cakes, this is universally popular with all our deli customers. We make this using locally brewed Wiper & True Milkshake Stout or Porter. It is deliciously squidgy and moist, and works brilliantly as a tea-time cake or as a pudding with some fresh berries on the side.

PREPARATION TIME: 20 MINUTES | BAKING TIME: 1 HOUR PLUS COOLING TIME | SERVES: 10-12

METHOD

For the cake

Preheat the oven to 150°C. Grease and line a 23cm spring-form cake tin.

Pour the stout into a saucepan and heat on a moderate heat until simmering. Add the cubed butter and gently stir until melted. Once the butter has melted, add the cocoa powder and caster sugar to the pan. Whisk vigorously until the ingredients are well combined and the mixture is smooth, and leave on the hob to simmer for 5 minutes.

Whilst the stout mixture is simmering, beat the eggs, yoghurt and vanilla extract together until they are well combined. Sieve the flour and bicarbonate of soda into a large bowl, add the ground almonds and stir through to mix.

Take the saucepan off the heat. Add the egg mixture to the saucepan and fold together until well mixed. Make a well in the flour and pour and scrape the stout mix into the well. Fold everything together until smooth. If there are any lumps in the mix, break them down using a hand whisk.

Pour the mixture into the prepared cake tin and bake for approximately 1 hour. Test the cake with a skewer or knife – the cake is very moist so the skewer doesn't need to be completely dry or clean when it comes out, but it shouldn't have uncooked cake mixture stuck to it. Leave the cake to cool in its tin.

Once the cake is cool, take it out of its tin, remove the greaseproof paper and sit it on a serving plate.

For the topping

Empty the mascarpone into a bowl and stir briefly to loosen. Sieve the icing sugar into the bowl and mix until smooth. If you have a hand-whisk or can do this in an electric mixer it will make the job quicker and ensure a smooth icing. Add a dash of vanilla bean paste or extract and mix through. Spread the mascarpone mix on top of the cake and decorate as you wish! We leave it plain and simple, resembling a glass of stout.

INGREDIENTS

For the cake:

250ml Wiper & True Milkshake Stout or Porter (or other good-quality stout or porter)
250g unsalted butter, cut into cubes, plus a little extra for greasing the tin
75g cocoa powder
350g caster sugar
2 large free-range eggs
150ml natural yoghurt (we use Yeo Valley)
1 tsp vanilla extract (we use Little Pod)
200g plain flour
2½ tsp bicarbonate of soda
75g ground almonds

For the topping:

250g mascarpone
60g icing sugar
A dash of vanilla bean paste or vanilla extract

"Everything just
seems that
little bit
better with
cake."

The Mall Deli

MILL KITCHEN

Your Friendly Neighbourhood Kitchen

Welcome to Mill Kitchen – a laidback café serving up great food made with quality ingredients.

MILL KITCHEN
1 The Old Combing
Sunny Bank Mills
Farsley
LS28 5UJ

Telephone:
0113 257 1417

Website:
www.millkitchen.
co.uk

Relaxed cafe/
deli for brunch,
lunch, coffee and
cake. Friendly
to vegetarians,
vegans, gluten–
free folk, bicycles,
dogs and children.

Take a look beyond the city centre, and you'll find a plethora of community-driven, local heroes that challenge some of the city's finest establishments in terms of quality and value for money. Mill Kitchen, run by husband and wife team Tom and Ailsa, is one of those places and you'll find it in Farsley's historic Sunny Bank Mills, a heritage site with decades in the textile industry behind it. Just like the original mill, Mill Kitchen is all about using great raw materials and traditional methods to produce the best results.

"We believe strongly in honest wholesome food: food that is made with traceable, sustainable ingredients and made with care, is food that will do you good. Everything is fresh and healthy, nothing is processed and we don't take any short cuts!" says Ailsa. Most goods are made from scratch on site but things that aren't are brought in from local people that they trust, such as Leeds Bread Co-op, North Star Coffee, Cryer & Stott Cheese and Northern Bloc Ice Cream.

The Mill Kitchen chefs use the seasonal produce on offer to inspire a regularly changing menu which features plenty of substantial brunch options as well as lunch plates, skillet dishes, nourishing bowls and a daily range of fresh salads. The Mill Kitchen philosophy is all about balance, so you'll also find a wide array of baked goods expertly turned out by their team of skilled bakers. Vegetarians and vegans are well catered for and there are plenty of gluten and dairy-free options too, making it easy for everyone to eat well.

As well as offering good quality grub, Mill Kitchen prides itself on supporting local talent. You'll find the vibrant space filled with a range of cook books, fair trade homeware and art produced by local artists. So, while waiting for your sourdough toast fix, you can browse the shelves for anything that takes your fancy.

The café has a great family atmosphere, providing plenty of space for pushchairs and always welcoming a visit from your furry friends. With exciting plans to expand in the pipeline, including extra kitchen space and an outdoor terrace, there'll be more tasty bakes up for grabs soon, and even more room for you to bring the whole family around for a wholesome, delicious meal.

If you haven't visited Farsley, or the Mill Kitchen, a warm welcome awaits.

Mill Kitchen
Raspberry Cheesecake Brownie

This is an amalgamation of our original brownie, adapted from a Hugh Fearnley-Whittingstall recipe and a cheesecake swirl brownie, which we've made gluten-free. The browned butter and high level of cocoa makes it incredibly rich and the cheesecake, with its subtle tang of goat's cheese, sets it off perfectly. You can use any seasonal fruit – blackcurrants & cherries are also delicious.

PREPARATION TIME: 30 MINUTES | BAKING TIME: 45 MINUTES | SERVES: 12-16

INGREDIENTS

For the fruit:
1 tbsp brandy
150g raspberries

For the brownie:
180g butter
3 eggs
300g light brown sugar
1 tsp vanilla extract
100g cocoa powder
50g ground almonds
Pinch of salt
100g dark chocolate, chopped

For the cheesecake:
240g cream cheese
120g goat's cheese, mild
30g butter
1 egg
45g caster sugar

METHOD

For the fruit
Start by stirring the brandy into the raspberries; leave them to macerate while you prepare the brownie mixture.

For the brownie
Preheat the oven to 180°c and grease a 24 by 24cm square tin with butter.

Brown the butter over a high heat in a saucepan; you are looking for it to go a golden brown colour and smell nutty and delicious (rather than just like hot melted butter). Keep an eye on it as it can bubble over easily! Meanwhile, beat the eggs and sugar together in a food mixer or with an electric whisk until the mixture is thick and pale and starting to hold its shape as it leaves the whisk. When the butter is ready, take it off the heat and add the vanilla. Pour this into the egg and sugar mix and beat it all together. In a separate bowl whisk together the cocoa powder, ground almonds and salt to remove any lumps. Add the dry ingredients to the wet and combine well (you can be quite vigorous). Finally, stir in the chocolate and pour the brownie mixture into the tin.

For the cheesecake
For the cheesecake mix, beat everything together (again this is easier with a food mixer or electric whisk) until thick and smooth. Fold in the raspberries just enough to get a ripple effect. Spoon the cheesecake mixture over the brownie and swirl together with the point of a knife.

Bake in the oven for 30 to 45 minutes; as it's quite a wet mixture it will take longer and look more cooked than a typical brownie - you want it to be set and not wobbly when you take it out.

This brownie is best served chilled; it will keep in the fridge for approximately 5 days.

"We believe strongly in honest wholesome food: food that is made with traceable, sustainable ingredients and made with care, is food that will do you good. Everything is fresh and healthy, nothing is processed and we don't take any short cuts!"

Tom and Ailsa, owners, Mill Kitchen

PINKMANS

A 21st Century Bakery

Pinkmans is a celebration of everything that made traditional bakeries great, while challenging conceptions of what a bakery on the modern high street can be…a cocktail with your cake perhaps?

Pinkmans is a place where old meets new. Traditions are cherished while new ideas are explored. At its heart is a bakery – the oven forms the very soul of the business, and it is from the onsite oven where bread starts emerging from 8am.

Opening its doors in December 2015, Pinkmans is a collaboration between long-time bakers and pastry chefs Steven Whibley, Troels Bendix and Michael Engler. In Steven's words, the business is an expression of what a modern high street bakery can be. "The buzz and energy at Pinkmans comes from making and baking everything in the same space as we sell it. In most places where you buy your bread, the bakers are non-existent, being packed off in some production facility that may make things easier but loses the excitement and passion that comes with wild yeast baking, Pinkmans is our attempt to change that."

It might not look like a typical bakery but at the heart of the business are bakers... and lots and lots of baking. Pizzas, fresh bread, sandwiches, cakes and tarts are all eaten around sharing tables, which contributes to the irresistible buzz and vibrant atmosphere. The team are certainly passionate about what they do, always eager to help and engage with the customers; there's a warmth to the atmosphere that has nothing to do with the baker's oven.

PINKMANS
85 Park Street
Bristol BS1 5PJ

Telephone:
0117 403 2040

Website:
www.pinkmans.
co.uk

Breaking with
bakery tradition.

Pinkmans
Apple Crumble Cake with Cinnamon Ice Cream

INGREDIENTS

For the cinnamon ice cream:
1 litre whole milk
75g fresh ginger, peeled and finely chopped
10g ground cinnamon
1 vanilla pod, split
½ orange, zest
8 egg yolks
125g light soft brown sugar

For the apple purée:
4 Granny Smith apples, cored and finely chopped
30g caster sugar
2g malic acid (available online)

For the wholemeal crumble:
250g wholemeal flour
100g plain flour
100g porridge oats
80g light brown sugar
2g cinnamon, 1g ground nutmeg, 1g clove powder
160g butter

For the cake:
2 Bramley apples, peeled, cored and diced
50g pecans and 50g dried apple, chopped
50g sultanas
30ml brandy
10ml lemon juice
60g granulated sugar, 160g Demerara sugar
2 medium eggs
150g unsalted butter, melted
200g plain flour
6g baking powder
3g salt, 3g ground cinnamon, 2g ground nutmeg, 1g clove powder

This is an old favourite that works well hot or cold, eaten alone or even better we think served warm with cinnamon ice cream. The crumble is a great topping for muffins or sweet brioches, too.

PREPARATION TIME: 15 MINUTES | BAKING TIME: 1 HOUR 40 MINUTES, PLUS 5 HOURS INFUSING | SERVES: 4

METHOD

For the cinnamon ice cream
Place the milk in a pan and bring to a simmer. Remove from the heat and add the ginger, cinnamon, vanilla pod and orange zest. Cover and leave to infuse for 60 minutes. Then pass through a fine sieve to remove the aromatics. Return to the heat and bring to a simmer. Whisk together the egg yolks and sugar in a bowl and then pour the hot milk mixture over and whisk to combine. Return to the pan and continue to heat gently, stirring continuously, until the mixture coats the back of a spoon. Remove from the heat and pass through a fine sieve. Chill in the fridge for 2 hours. Pour the chilled mixture into a plastic container with a secure lid and place in the freezer. Remove every 1 hour and stir to encourage an even freezing and reduce ice crystals. Repeat until the mixture is of a soft-scoop ice cream consistency.

For the apple purée
Place the apples, sugar and malic acid in a pan and cover with a lid. Place on the stove and cook on a medium heat for 10 minutes, then remove the lid and continue cooking until soft and broken down. Purée in a food processor. Set aside.

For the wholemeal crumble
Preheat the oven to 170°C. Combine the dry ingredients in a food mixer fitted with the paddle attachment and then add the butter and rub to a crumb. Place in a baking tray and bake the mix for about 45 minutes, rubbing through the mixture every 15 minutes to avoid large lumps. Set aside.

For the cake
Preheat the oven to 190°C. Grease and line a 25cm square cake tin. Place the diced apples, chopped pecans, chopped dried apple and sultanas into a mixing bowl, then add the brandy and lemon juice and leave to macerate for 30 minutes. In a food mixer fitted with the whisk attachment, whip the sugars and the eggs for 4 minutes. Then add the melted butter, then the flour, baking powder, salt, cinnamon, nutmeg and clove powder. Finally, add the macerated fruit and nuts. Bake for about 40 minutes or until firm to the touch and golden. Then cover the top with the apple purée and top with the wholemeal crumble. Allow to cool, then portion and serve with the cinnamon ice cream.

PROPERMAID
Bank Bottom
Works
Marsh Garden
Huddersfield
West Yorkshire
HD9 6AP

Telephone:
01484 766068

Website:
www.propermaid.
co.uk

Uniquely fabulous
'proper' cakes
and baked
products that are
competitively
priced and
supported
by friendly,
professional
service.

INGREDIENTS

For the sponge:
185g self-raising flour
105g soft vegetable
margarine, preferably
80% fat content
185g caster sugar
25g cocoa powder
5g bicarbonate of soda
85ml milk
165ml dandelion &
burdock pop (half a can)
2 eggs

For the icing:
20g vegetable
margarine, softened
130g icing sugar
10g cocoa powder
20ml dandelion &
burdock pop

ProperMaid
Dandelion and Burdock Cake

This recipe was developed as a tribute to Huddersfield using the iconic Ben Shaws brand. It became our signature cake and has gone on to win two awards – best bakery product at the Deliciously Yorkshire Awards and a gold star at the Great Taste Awards 2011. We still sell this cake today and it's now one of our top ten bestselling cakes!

PREPARATION TIME: 30 MINUTES | BAKING TIME: 45 MINUTES | SERVES: 8

METHOD

For the sponge
Preheat the oven at 160°c/Gas 3. Grease and line a 18cm, round spring-form cake tin.

Rub together the flour, margarine, caster sugar, cocoa powder and bicarbonate of soda until it resembles fine breadcrumbs. Gradually add the milk and the dandelion & burdock pop (reserving 20ml for the icing) followed by the eggs. Beat together until a thick smooth batter consistency is achieved.

Pour the cake batter into the cake tin and bake in the oven for approximately 40 minutes until it is firm to the touch and when inserted with a cake skewer comes out clean.

For the icing
Beat together the soft margarine and icing sugar until smooth. Add the cocoa powder and dandelion & burdock pop you reserved earlier and mix until well combined. Spread onto the flat side of the cake and sprinkle with some icing sugar to serve!

Explore
Eat And Enjoy

Set within the grounds of The Dartington Hall Estate, The Shops at Dartington is a social enterprise with something for everyone, from crafts & gifts to delicious food & drink.

THE SHOPS AT DARTINGTON

Shinner's Bridge
Dartington
Devon TQ9 6TQ

Telephone:
01803 847500

Website:
www.dartington.
org/shops

The Shops at Dartington comprise 14 shops, cafes and workshops, which includes a locally sourced food hall run as a social enterprise and located on the beautiful Dartington Hall Estate.

The Dartington Hall Trust, a registered charity, is a place that offers opportunities to experiment with living a larger and more connected life: to discover our true potential and pioneer meaningful change in ourselves and society. This approach is inspired by the vision of the founders, which is being reinvented to meet the challenge of a new time.

The Shops at Dartington grew out of the original farm shop on the estate 40 years ago. The historic farm buildings became home to the shops and cafés in this picturesque rural spot, which is just two miles outside of Totnes. Over the last four decades, they have grown slowly and organically into today's eclectic collection of shops and eateries. The collection includes a kitchen shop, craft gallery, pottery workshop, fashion and beauty stores, a Dartington crystal gallery, homeware, stationery, gifts, toys, clothing, food and drink.

There is a focus on all things Devon, especially in the food and drink offerings. The huge food hall is jam-packed with West Country produce from small producers; 87% of the products are made in the West Country, and an impressive 60% are from Devon itself. The fresh section is stocked with locally grown salads, artisan breads, cakes, tarts, savoury pastries, West Country cheeses and organic milk, butter, cream and yoghurts.

As far as the store cupboard goes, there is no end to the options! Jams, chutneys and curds are made using local artisan makers for The Shops at Dartington's own brand; popcorn, crisps and nuts come from various local producers; handmade cakes, biscuits and cookies are made by small Devon bakers; and there is a range of pasta, rice, spices, oils, sauces and tinned food, as well as plentiful sugar-free, dairy-free and gluten-free items.

For drinks, Devon Drinks is a treasure trove of artisan drinks from the region, including Dartington's very own Elmhirst Gin. A celebration of locally produced wines, ales, ciders, beers, spirits and soft drinks, this charming new shop is actually based within the historic apple store building – a truly fitting location considering the gorgeous West Country ciders it stocks!

The two cafés on site are passionate about local sourcing and quality ingredients. Surrounded by beautiful countryside and with so much delicious local produce available, there is no better place to sample a true taste of Devon.

The Shops at Dartington
Passion Curd Cake

This cake is taken to new heights with a zingy passionfruit curd from Dartington and butter icing filling. Cut open a fresh passionfruit and drizzle it over the top for extra wow factor.

PREPARATION TIME: 20 MINUTES | BAKING TIME: 20 MINUTES | SERVES: 8

METHOD

For the cake

Preheat the oven to 180°c. Grease two 20cm sandwich cake tins. Beat the caster sugar and butter together in a mixing bowl until pale and creamy. Beat the eggs in a separate bowl, then add them slowly to the sugar and butter mixture. If it starts to look like it is curdling, add a tablespoon of the flour. Fold in the remaining flour with the baking powder and add the vanilla extract. Divide the mixture between the two greased cake tins and level them off with a spatula. Place them in the oven for about 20 minutes or until the cake springs back when gently pressed and is golden brown. Leave to cool in the tins for 10 minutes, then turn out onto a wire rack to cool completely.

For the butter icing

Put all the butter icing ingredients into a mixing bowl and beat together until smooth.

For the filling and decoration

Place one of the cakes on a stand or plate and spread a layer of passionfruit curd onto it. Add a thin layer of butter icing and top with the second cake. Decorate the top with a layer of passionfruit curd and pipe butter icing around the edge of the cake. Finish with some fresh passionfruit, if you like.

INGREDIENTS

For the cake:

225g caster sugar
225g butter
4 large eggs
225g self-raising flour
2 tsp baking powder
Dash of good-quality vanilla extract

For the butter icing:

225g butter
100g icing sugar
1-2 tsp milk

For the filling and decoration:

Dartington passion fruit curd, for spreading
1 passionfruit (optional)

SLATTERY

Naughty, But Incredibly nice...

Family-run Slattery offers a classic triple-threat: the UK's best handmade chocolatier, they also make outstanding celebration cakes and specialise in traditional afternoon teas.

SLATTERY
197 Bury New Road
Whitefield, Bury
M45 6GE

Telephone:
0161 7679303

Website:
www.slattery.
co.uk

A family-run business stretching back over three generations and half a century, Slattery offers incredible handmade chocolates, pastries, cakes, celebration pieces and afternoon teas.

A day without chocolate is, essentially, a day wasted and no good meal is complete without that wonderful bit at the end where you say "I shouldn't, but...oh, go on then." Luckily for the residents of Manchester (and beyond) this is the area that Slattery, based in their imposing three-storey Victorian building in Whitefield, have excelled in for over 51 years. They're that rare thing in modern business: a three-generations deep family-run firm who've established a stellar reputation for all things sweet, sticky, and delicious on a simple ethos: make the best chocolates, pastries, cakes, bakes, biscuits, scones and teas from the best produce drawing on the best of their expertise, knowledge and traditions.

Everything is made on the premises, from the bespoke celebration and wedding cakes to the handmade chocolates, the fresh cream cakes, fancies and ice creams, which are available over-the-counter and alongside a range of gifts in the ground floor retail shop. The bread is baked fresh daily and is so good that it finds its way to other local outlets right across Manchester. The elegant and imposing Mason's Dining Room, on the second floor, offers a fantastic daytime dining from freshly-made sandwiches and afternoon teas all the way through to made-on-the-premises desserts.

With Slattery the proof of the pudding is most definitely in the eating. Jo, one of the third-generation of the family to work in the business, takes up the story. "From the original bakery, we developed the confectionery side of the business, and every few years we seemed to outgrow our premises. By 2004, John Slattery had set his sights on the Mason's Arms, a derelict local landmark directly opposite our premises on Bury New Road. The family completely refurbished it, and kept adding to it as the business kept growing. We want our customers to be able to sit and enjoy good food, or pop in to pick up their daily bread, or drop by to discuss cake, confectionery or catering for their most special events."

As with the produce, the devil is in the detail. Visitors can watch the production processes via specially installed windows and the bravest can take on the awesome chocolate challenge: an American Fudge Sundae Cake lathered in cream and chocolate sauce. Manage to clean your plate and the prize is... more chocolate!

Luckily for the citizens of Manchester (and the rest of us) it looks like Slattery will be continuing into a fourth generation and will be here for us for a long time to come.

Slattery Manchester Tart with Chocolate

A staple during its heyday on the school dinner menu in the 1970s and 1980s, this is a fantastic twist on the classic traditional Manchester tart.

PREPARATION TIME: 20 MINUTES | BAKING TIME: 20 MINUTES | MAKES: 10 TARTS

METHOD

For the pastry

Cream the butter and sugar together until combined before adding the eggs one at a time, continuing to work the mixture. Sieve in the flour and mix to a paste. Be careful not to overwork the mixture. Then, wrap in plastic and chill/rest in the refrigerator for at least 30 minutes. Using a rolling pin on a lightly floured surface, roll out the pastry and line small tart cases, allowing them to rest back in the refrigerator to avoid shrinkage before blind baking them at 180°c for approximately 10 minutes.

For the filling

Whisk the eggs, sugar, vanilla and cornflour together to make a custard. Bring the milk to the boil before adding in the combined ingredients. Continue to heat for a few minutes whisking all the time. Removing the mixture from the heat, add the chocolate callets, stirring well until they dissolve.

To finish

Spread a little fruit jam or Nutella onto the baked pastry before pouring the chocolate custard over it. Be careful not to overfill the pastry cases. Allow to cool completely before adding chocolate flakes (or other sprinkles) to finish.

As an alternative, try adding fresh fruit such as strawberry halves to the jam before adding the custard. Then top with a strawberry half dipped in chocolate – decadent, but delicious!

To serve

These are fantastic on their own, of course, but to ramp up the indulgence, try serving with a rich vanilla clotted ice cream.

INGREDIENTS

For the pastry:
500g butter (or margarine)
200g caster sugar
4 whole eggs, medium
700g plain flour

For the filling:
3 whole eggs, medium
120g caster sugar
10g vanilla paste
40g cornflour
640g milk (full fat)
100g 70% chocolate Callets

To finish:
Fruit jam (or Nutella)
Chocolate flakes (or other chocolate decoration)

"Don't be put off by the thought of using chocolate in baking; it's much easier than you think!"

John, owner, Slattery

THAYMAR

Keeping It In The Family

Thaymar's luxury ice creams and sorbets are sold all over the UK, but the place that started it all also boasts a farm shop and tea room – tucked away in the Notts countryside.

THAYMAR ICE CREAM, FARM SHOP & TEA ROOM
Haughton Park Farm
Near Bothamsall
Retford
Notts DN22 8DB

Telephone: 01623 862632

Website: www.thaymaricecream.co.uk

Thaymar offers over 35 flavours of award-winning luxury ice cream and sorbet all made on site with natural ingredients.

Thaymar Ice Cream began back in the 1980s when Thelma and Martin Cheetham devised a tasty and profitable way to use up surplus milk from their dairy herd. Today, their children Emily and Thomas have pivotal roles in the day-to-day management of the business as a whole, along with Emily's husband Tom Woodcock, who heads up production. It would be remiss not to mention the contribution of Tom and Emily's own children too, who earned their pocket money at Thaymar's temporary picking station, gathering produce for the Belvoir cordial that flavours Thaymar's well-loved Elderflower and Gooseberry ice cream.

As you might imagine, they are a close knit team, though it's not just family who stick around – Zoe White joined Thaymar as a waitress whilst still at school, and is now the office manager. Customers are very much part of the clan at Thaymar too – some regulars visit every single day, which we reckon is almost a better endorsement than the multiple Great Taste awards the ice cream has picked up over the years. The business doesn't need to spend much time on advertising, as the reputation of the ice cream and the tea room travels mostly by word of mouth but the team certainly don't take that for granted.

They make a point of rewarding the effort their customers make to find them off the beaten track, by changing the tea room specials weekly, introducing brand new creations – the brilliant concept of a 'Yorkshire burrito' filled with slow-cooked beef brisket and roasted veg with chips on the side was a particular hit – and hosting off-the-cuff events such as murder mystery nights and gourmet dining experiences.

Expertly combining a very local and a nationwide appeal, Thaymar recently diversified into raising beef shorthorn and Hampshire Down sheep, which are butchered locally and brought back to head chef Jamie Manning, who has to get inventive in order to make use of every cut. Although Thaymar Ice Cream no longer has its own dairy herd, it still makes everything on site. This includes bespoke flavours developed to order, such as a mince pie ice cream for a pub planning their Christmas menu, and the 'Jess & John' ice cream – an espresso salted caramel flavour created for the eponymous couple's wedding day. With so many facets to the business, what unites Thaymar's talents is an ethos that Emily puts very simply: "whatever we do, it's got to be the best". Whether they're serving sorbet, sirloin steak or a Sunday roast, this family business seems to have passed down the secret formula to success!

Thaymar Ice Cream

Chocolate Orange Bread & Butter Pudding

The tea room staff are under strict orders from devoted customers to keep Emily's Christmas leftovers-inspired pudding on the menu at all times. Strangely enough, until she included 'chocolate orange' in the name, it hadn't sold at all – thank goodness people came to their senses, as we wouldn't want anyone to miss out on the chance to make this at home!

PREPARATION TIME: 15 MINUTES | BAKING TIME: 40 MINUTES | SERVES: 4

METHOD

Slice the panettone and layer the slices into a 22 x 28cm ovenproof dish, tucking chunks of chocolate into the layers between slices. In a small saucepan, gently melt the butter and cream until all the butter has melted. Make sure the mixture does not boil. Remove from the heat and add the orange juice and orange zest to the cream mixture.

In a separate bowl, whisk the eggs and sugar, then gradually add the cream mixture whilst whisking to get a nice smooth custard. Pour over the panettone slices, allowing the custard to soak through all of the layers. If time allows, refrigerate the pudding for 30 minutes as this will help the panettone soak up all the liquid.

Bake at 160°c for approximately 25 minutes until golden brown and set. Let it cool slightly, then sprinkle with Demerara sugar and chocolate curls.

To serve

We suggest serving a big slice of the warm, oozy pudding with Thaymar Brandy and Orange ice cream. Can you blame us?

INGREDIENTS

750g Italian panettone (or other fruity bread)
125g dark chocolate, broken into chunks
125g butter
400ml cream
300ml orange juice
3 oranges, zested
5 eggs
100g sugar
Sprinkle of Demerara sugar
Chocolate curls

"Whatever we do,
it's got to be
the best."

Emily, manager, Thaymar Ice Cream

TIFFIN TEAHOUSE

Time For Tea

Home-cooked meals and slices of freshly baked cake, all washed down with a pot of proper loose leaf tea...

TIFFIN TEAHOUSE
35 Abbey Road
West Bridgford
Nottingham
NG2 5NG

Telephone:
0115 981 6224

Website:
www.
tiffinteahouse.
uk.com

Offering a delicate slice of nostalgia alongside their afternoon teas, and traditional lunch and breakfast menus, Tiffin Teahouse focus on fresh, tasty, homemade food for customers of all ages.

Owners Jo Bounds and Diane Elliott shared a vision of providing all the welcoming traditions of a great British afternoon tea when they opened Tiffin Tea House back in 2011. The result is a timeless place for customers of all ages to enjoy food and drink that's freshly prepared, lovingly baked and carefully poured.

In the six years since its opening, Tiffin has established itself as a firm favourite within Nottingham, and for good reason. The pretty and welcoming interior, along with the inviting aroma of homemade goods, are just part of the charm, as the tight-knit team provide some of the city's friendliest service in a venue at the heart of its community. It's a formula so winning that Jo and Diane have recently had to expand Tiffin's premises, taking over neighbouring community venture Renew 37's space on Fridays, Saturdays and Sundays to create a bigger tea party for everyone.

It's safe to say the Tiffin team aren't afraid of a challenge; in 2016 they were chosen to cater for an event attended by Team GB's regional Olympic medal winners. The tea house is also a popular location for visiting film crews, which have included Come Dine With Me, Don't Tell The Bride and Location, Location, Location.

For Tiffin's loyal customers, the appeal lies in the tea house's delicious and honest food, its 'think local' mindset, its door-always-open approach to service and, of course, the cakes. Inventive flavours, showcased in the Cake of the Month, have included everything from pumpkin to peanut butter, and Tiffin is equally happy to cater for gluten-free guests with an impressively wide range of offerings to suit all tastes.

The cherry on top of this particularly perfect cake is Tiffin's unrivalled range of international teas, uniting the more traditional aspects of a time-honoured tea house with a modern, forward-thinking, community venue. We'll drink to that!

Tiffin Tea House Butterscotch Cake

A simple recipe for a shamelessly indulgent treat based on a classic British favourite. Perfect for sharing at celebrations, and sure to impress the guests.

PREPARATION TIME: 10 MINUTES | BAKING TIME: 20-25 MINUTES | SERVES: 10

METHOD

For the cake

Preheat the oven to 180°c and line two 20cm sandwich tins.

Cream the margarine and sugars together in a large bowl until light in texture and colour. Gradually beat in the eggs with a whisk, and then fold in the flour by hand. Once well combined, transfer the mixture to sandwich tins and bake for 20 to 25 minutes.

INGREDIENTS

For the cake:

250g margarine
100g caster sugar
150g soft brown sugar
5 eggs, beaten
250g self raising flour, sieved

For the butterscotch filling:

85g butter
50g soft brown sugar
50g golden syrup
350g icing sugar
2 tbsp milk

For the caramel topping:

25g butter
25g soft brown sugar
25g golden syrup
2 tbsp double cream
50g vanilla fudge pieces

For the butterscotch filling

In a small saucepan, melt the butter, sugar and syrup together until dissolved. Next, beat in the icing sugar and add enough milk to achieve spreading consistency. Leave to cool slightly.

Returning to the sponge, slice through it horizontally so you have four layers. Sandwich the layers together with the butterscotch filling.

For the caramel topping

Melt all the ingredients over a low heat and allow to bubble for 30 seconds. Leave to cool completely. Spoon the caramel over the layered sponges.

Decorate as desired with vanilla fudge, homemade or otherwise!

Tiffin Tea House Lime And Coconut Cake

This tropical cake is a popular feature of the Tiffin Tea House, created by owners Jo and Diane who turn out up to 22 delicious bakes every day! Follow their icing instructions carefully to reproduce the striking finish on this triple layered delight.

PREPARATION TIME: 10 MINUTES | BAKING TIME: 20-25 MINUTES | SERVES: 10

METHOD

Before beginning, ensure all the ingredients are at room temperature, and preheat the oven to 180°c (160°c for a fan oven). Grease and line three 20cm (8") round cake tins.

For the sponge

Cream the margarine and caster sugar until the mixture is light in colour. Gradually add the eggs, mixing thoroughly, then stir in the lime zest and coconut. Sift the flour and fold it in carefully to create an airy texture.

Divide the sponge mixture between the three prepared tins and bake in the preheated oven for approximately 20 minutes. Once cooked, leave the cakes in the tins to cool slightly, then remove them from the tins to cool completely.

For the coconut cream filling

Warm the creamed coconut and then beat it with the coconut oil until they are combined and the mixture is soft. Add half of the icing sugar and all the milk or water, mix thoroughly and then add the remaining icing sugar.

For the decoration

Next, make up the glacé icing using the lime juice and enough icing sugar for a smooth but not too runny consistency. In a separate bowl, gradually add green food colouring to the desiccated coconut and keep mixing with a fork until all the pieces are the desired colour.

To assemble

Set aside approximately one third of the coconut cream for the sides and piping, and layer the three cakes with coconut cream and lime marmalade. Once the sponges are firmly in place, evenly coat the sides with the remaining coconut cream. Place the green desiccated coconut on a plate and carefully roll the sides of the cake in the coconut. Fill an icing bag with the last of the coconut cream and pipe stars around the top edge of the cake (we use a number eight piping tube for this) to form a barrier all the way round. Finally, flood the top of the cake with the lime glacé icing and finish with an extra sprinkling of green coconut pieces.

INGREDIENTS

For the sponge:

250g margarine (Stork is our preference)
250g caster sugar
5 eggs
1 lime, zested
25g unsweetened desiccated coconut
250g self-raising flour

For the filling:

100g pure creamed coconut
250g coconut oil
400g icing sugar
50ml milk (or water, if you prefer)
150g lime marmalade

For the icing and decoration:

1 lime, juiced
Icing sugar
Green food colouring
40g desiccated coconut

WALK MILL

A Miller's Tale

Walk Mill is a water mill set in the Cheshire countryside with a fascinating history as well as an enticing café and shop selling flour, cakes and loaves. It's a real gem with plenty to explore.

When the Jones family uncovered the remains of a 13th-century mill on their family-run arable farm, they set about the daunting task of bringing it back to life. After much hard work, Ben Jones and his family rebuilt the mill on the ancient foundations and have now been producing stone-ground flour there for over seven years.

The area is a perfect spot for a stroll around the Cheshire countryside, with centuries-old footpaths criss-crossing the farmland. Despite the mill being at the heart of this walker's paradise, the name Walk Mill actually came from its original history as a fuller's mill (cloth mill) and the 'walkers' whose job it was to clean the cloth.

WALK MILL
Walk Mill Lane
Waverton,
Chester
Cheshire
CH3 7BF

Telephone:
01829 749373

Water mill stone-grinding home-grown wheat to make flour, which is used to bake goods for the on-site cafe and sold for wholesale and retail.

This is just part of the intriguing history discovered by the Jones family as they pieced together the story of their mill. The original floor tiles have been given a new lease of life in the Miller's Kitchen and mill area and hand-made bricks that were excavated can be seen surrounding the fireplace. The original sack hoist and damsel have also been put back to use in the mill today.

All this attention to tradition and heritage doesn't stop with the building's structure, of course. The stone-ground flour is all made from an English wheat variety grown in the fields surrounding the mill (no food miles!), which is slowly stone-ground from whole grains to preserve all the nutrients.

The different grades on offer – wholemeal, white and malted – are created by various levels of sifting. No bleaching is involved and each grade makes fantastic cakes, bread and pastry. Just pop into our café, The Miller's Kitchen, to taste the products with a cup of tea!

Freshly made goodies are on offer every day in this popular on-site café, from sandwiches, toasties and soups to flapjack, scones and cakes. Of course, whole loaves are available to buy along with the flour itself so that you can whip up tasty treats in your own kitchen. The flour is already being used by renowned restaurants across Cheshire, and is available at many of our county's retailers and farm shops, too.

Walk Mill Wholemeal Scones

Using our Walk Mill stone-ground wholemeal flour gives the scones a nice texture and earthy flavour due to the bran. People are always surprised about how light these are, and this is due to the addition of natural yoghurt, which is our secret ingredient!

PREPARATION TIME: 10 MINUTES | BAKING TIME: 15-20 MINUTES | SERVES: 9

METHOD
Preheat the oven to 220°C.

Put the flour, butter, sugar, baking powder and salt into a mixing bowl and rub the butter in until the mixture is the consistency of breadcrumbs.

Add the egg, sultanas, golden syrup and yoghurt, and mix again until a wet dough is formed.
Turn out onto a flour-dusted work surface. Flatten out to about 2cm in depth then cut out about 9 scones with a fluted scone cutter. Place the scones on a baking tray lined with baking parchment.
Bake in the preheated oven for approximately 15 to 20 minutes until the scones are golden brown and 'bounce' back if pressed down.

INGREDIENTS
450g Walk Mill Stone-ground Wholemeal Flour
125g butter
1 tbsp caster sugar
2 tsp baking powder
½ tsp salt
1 egg
50g sultanas
1 tbsp golden syrup
250g natural yoghurt

WALKER'S NURSERIES

Business Is Blooming

The family-run garden centre and restaurant Walker's Nurseries is a place where beautiful plants and plates are celebrated side by side.

Walker's Nurseries began life in 1951 when Lawrence and Vera Walker purchased the plot of land outside Blaxton, Doncaster, and began growing roses. Today the business is still run with the same love and care by the Walker family.

WALKER'S NURSERIES
Mosham Road
Blaxton
Doncaster
DN9 3BA

Telephone:
01302 770325

Website: www. walkers nurseries.tv

Garden centre/ plant nursery with a gift shop, restaurant and landscaped gardens.

The heritage of the family business is honoured in the spirit of the centre. The stunning landscaped gardens feature plenty of roses, and the petals find their way into some of the dishes too – such as in the ever-popular rose and lemon sponge, which is a favourite on the menu.

Their gardening displays have won countless awards over the years and the family is proud of their inventive creations, which they hope can inspire gardeners all over the region. In 2012 they expanded to open a new gift shop and 'food to go' section, containing a deli and bakery. Freshly made scones and cakes fill the bakery with irresistible aromas each day, and the deli is packed with Yorkshire products such as chutneys, jams and preserves.

One of the most special products on sale is the honey from their very own bee hives. People can even do bee experience courses on-site and learn about these precious little honey-makers.

The restaurant is the perfect place to try some hearty homemade food. Everything is made from scratch using local produce where possible. Morning guests can enjoy award-winning sausages in their Yorkshire breakfasts and lunch-time diners have a whole host of snacks and hot meals to choose from – the steak and ale pie (made with hand-made pastry) is their most popular dish. Sweet delights are also enjoyed with tea and coffee, including classic cream teas and luxurious afternoon teas. Not forgetting their famous Sunday roasts, which always feature free-range or outdoor-reared meat sourced from less than 30 miles away.

With The Potting Shed function room now available, people can also come to Walker's Nurseries to host their special parties and events. The room holds up to 45 people in a light, bright and welcoming space.

Walker's Nurseries Key Lime Cake

This classic American dessert is traditionally made with Key limes from the Florida Keys, but it is now a popular pud all over the world – and this Walker's Nurseries version, created by our chef Mark, never fails to please.

PREPARATION TIME: 30 MINUTES | BAKING TIME: 30 MINUTES, PLUS 6 HOURS CHILLING TIME | SERVES: 10-12

INGREDIENTS

For the sponge:
225g caster sugar
225g butter, softened
4 large eggs
275g self-raising flour
1 tsp baking powder
4 tbsp milk
2 limes, zest

For the filling:
4 large egg yolks
397ml tin condensed milk
5 limes, zest and juice
300ml double cream

To decorate:
Whipped cream
Lime wedges

METHOD

For the sponge
Preheat the oven to 170°c. Grease and base-line two 25cm loose-bottom spring-form cake tins with greaseproof paper.

Put the sugar and butter in a large bowl. Cream the two ingredients using an electric hand mixer or stand mixer until the mixture is pale and creamy. Add the eggs one at a time. Sieve the flour and baking powder together into a separate bowl, then add to the mixture along with the milk and lime zest. Beat for 2 minutes until well incorporated and you have a smooth batter.

Spoon the mixture evenly between the two cake tins and bake in the preheated oven for 25 to 30 minutes, until golden on top and firm to the touch. Leave in the cake tins to cool completely.

For the filling
While the sponge is cooling, make the filling. Place the egg yolks, condensed milk and lime juice into a bowl and mix together. Once fully incorporated the mix should thicken.

In a separate bowl whip the cream until ribbons start to form. Be careful not to over-whip the cream, as it will be too thick to mix into the lime mixture. Fold the cream into the lime mixture with the lime zest using a metal spoon.

To assemble and decorate
To assemble the cake, leave one layer of the cake in its tin. Spoon three-quarters of the lime mixture onto this cake layer and smooth over to completely cover the cake. Remove the greaseproof paper from the other cake, turn the cake upside-down so you have a flat top, and place this sponge layer on the lime mixture. Use the rest of the lime mixture to cover the cake, smoothing it with a palette knife. Chill the cake in the fridge for at least 6 hours, but preferably overnight. Remove from cake carefully from the tin. Decorate with whipped cream rosettes and lime wedges.

THE WATERMILL

Flour Power

THE WATERMILL
Little Salkeld
Penrith
Cumbria
CA10 1NN

Telephone:
01768 881 523

Website:
www.organicmill.
co.uk

18th century
watermill milling
organic and
biodynamic
stone-ground
British flours,
with a vegetarian
tearoom and
shop selling mill
produce, organic
groceries and
giftware, easily
found ten minutes
from Junction 40
of the M6 in the
picturesque Eden
Valley.

The Watermill is one of the few working mills in Britain that still uses water power, and probably the only one that's pink!

With tours, a vegetarian tea room, and a shop selling the mill produce as well as organic produce and giftware in the picturesque surroundings of Little Salkeld in the Eden Valley – The Watermill has something for everyone.

Current owners Phil and Cheryl have run The Watermill with Cheryl's son Elliot since 2014, after spending six months learning the ropes from previous owners. Along with the know-how to work in the mill and create longstanding favourite recipes from the flour produced, the couple also inherited the signature pink colour of the mill buildings, which were painted on their restoration in the 1970s. Today, the mill, the shop, and tea room enjoy regular local custom with the help of the staff that Cheryl trains herself in the art of traditional bread-making and other valuable skills.

The mill itself specialises in British flour, which is stone-ground to retain the nutrition and flavour that can be damaged by the heat of modern milling methods. They only use grains that are biodynamic – which is a stricter version of organic certification – and all from wheat, barley, rye and spelt sourced from just three British farms. The lower gluten content of the flours, because they're from British-grown grain rather than the foreign varieties used in commercial breads, makes them more suitable for everyone, and great tasting too of course!

The Watermill's flour (as well as oats, oatmeal and muesli) is sold in the onsite shop and also made into cakes, scones, bread and more for the vegetarian food served in the welcoming café. Other outlets from North Cumbria down to Manchester, including farm shops and health food shops, also sell The Watermill's products so you don't have to be nearby to sample a taste of the tradition and time-honoured knowledge that goes into the milling of these natural ingredients. Whether you're walking or cycling the Coast to Coast route, visiting the nearby 4000 year old stone circle, or just fancy a hot drink and a freshly baked treat, The Watermill is a great place to stop off or enjoy a day out. For those interested in the techniques used by this traditional working mill there are tours, and you can even learn how to perfect your own loaves with bread-making classes using The Watermill's products at Keswick Cookery School.

The Watermill Fruit Scones

Our scones are made using our 85% self-raising flour. Once the grain has been stone-ground in our mill, we sieve off most of the bran (the outer layers of the grain) to produce a lighter wholemeal flour. The reduced bran content makes for better baking but still leaves plenty of nutrition, colour and most importantly, flavour!

PREPARATION TIME: 10 MINUTES | BAKING TIME: 13-14 MINUTES | MAKES ABOUT 6 SCONES

METHOD
Mix the flour and sugar in a mixing bowl then rub the margarine into the flour and sugar with your fingertips. Then add the sultanas, or alternative dried fruit.

In a separate bowl, beat the eggs and mix in the yogurt and milk. Add enough of the wet ingredients to the flour, sugar and butter to make a soft dough; there should be a little bit left which you can use later in the recipe.

On a floured surface, pat the dough with your hand to flatten to a height slightly lower than the scone cutter. Cut out rounds and place on a lightly floured baking tray.

Brush the tops with the remaining egg, milk and yogurt mixture then bake the scones at 180°c for 13 to 14 minutes.

To serve
Slice in half and add butter, jam and/or cream to your liking!

INGREDIENTS
454g Watermill self-raising flour
28g cane sugar
113g margarine or sunflower spread
56g sultanas, soaked in warm orange juice (or similar amount of your choice of dried fruit)
2 eggs
2 tbsp plain yogurt
118ml whole milk

"Our secret
is simple,
quality
ingredients."

Elliot, baker, The Watermill

WELBECK BAKEHOUSE

An Estate Of Mind

WELBECK ESTATE
Welbeck
Worksop
Nottinghamshire
S80 3LW
A traditional landed estate in a beautiful rural location.

WELBECK BAKEHOUSE
Lower Motor Yard
Telephone:
01909 500 129
Website:
www.welbeck bakehouse.co.uk
Bakery using traditional fermentation methods to produce an incredible range of artisanal bread and pastries.

WELBECK FARM SHOP
The Courtyard
Telephone:
01909 478 725
Website:
www.welbeck farmshop.co.uk
One of the country's best farm shops, with a focus on low food miles and artisanal produce.

The Welbeck Bakehouse is an award-winning artisan bakery specialising in sourdough, ciabatta & viennoiserie on the Welbeck Estate, where the Welbeck Farm Shop has been selling fresh, quality produce for over a decade.

Firing up the ovens in 2008, The Welbeck Bakehouse built its foundations on a passion for creating and promoting 'Real Bread'. Avid supporters of The Real Bread Campaign, and inspired by a hunger to improve the day-to-day quality of nutrition the bakery has grown at an impressive rate to supply an array of independent businesses throughout Nottinghamshire, Yorkshire and Lincolnshire. The team never add artificial additives or improvers, and take immense pride in producing a multitude of delicious baked goods using preferments and slow fermentation methods. As a business, The Welbeck Bakehouse is passionate about sourcing locally and organically wherever possible. This even includes using produce from other businesses based on the Welbeck Estate.

Mark Garry heads up the whole operation, overseeing the extremely hard-working and talented bakers, delivery drivers and administrative teams who all contribute to the seven day-a-week business. This dedication to creating such high quality products has united a bakery team from all walks of life, and all the bakers are extremely involved with each stage of the process, from hand-scaling each product to dreaming up new seasonal specialities.

The Welbeck Bakehouse delivers freshly baked products to the Welbeck Farm Shop and Harley Cafe daily. The farm shop ensures that everything on the shelves or behind the counters is a product it is proud to sell, reflected in multiple Great Taste awards and a reputation as one of the country's best farm shops. Its cooperative relationship with the land is central to its success; the philosophy for sourcing products is 'start local' which is evidenced by the venison and game larder, stocked with the results of shoots on the estate. Seasonal produce and some very well-fed Welbeck pigs mean the farm shop is close to being a zero-waste business, as well as having very few food miles on the clock.

Manager Oliver Stubbins and his team work closely with everyone who supplies the farm shop, and even ask for taste-testing volunteers from the estate. Many of the staff are also locals, and have worked at the farm shop for as many years as it's been open. Regular customers know them well, and enjoy the kind of service, friendly interaction and knowledgeable guidance that you'd struggle to find in a supermarket: for the freshest and highest quality produce, the Welbeck Estate has it all.

The Welbeck Bakehouse

Welbeck Bakehouse
Lemon & Poppy Seed Brioche Swirls

The bakers at Welbeck Bakehouse developed this recipe as a seasonal product, to not only celebrate seasonal flavours but also to allow them a chance to create something new! Showcasing the potential of brioche as a delicious sweet treat, rather than just a plain bun, head baker Jack Arkless recommends serving these with homemade lemon curd and clotted cream.

PREPARATION TIME: 30 MINUTES, PLUS 10-12 HOURS RESTING AND 1-2 HOURS PROOFING |
BAKING TIME: 15-20 MINUTES | SERVES: 7

INGREDIENTS

For the brioche:

200g whole eggs
100g milk
500g type 00 flour
15g fresh yeast
7½g salt
125g softened butter, cut into small cubes
55g caster sugar
1 lemon, zested and juiced
100g poppy seeds

For the icing:

500g icing sugar
2 tsp cold water
1 tsp lemon juice

METHOD

In a large bowl combine the whole eggs and milk, then add the flour, yeast and salt. Mix until the dough comes together, then knead for a further 15 to 20 minutes. If using an electric mixer, mix on a slow speed for 2 to 3 minutes using the dough hook attachment and then on a medium/fast speed for a further 6 to 8 minutes. At this point the dough should be soft, glossy and elastic.

Now add half the butter and half the sugar, mix for 4 to 5 minutes to incorporate both into the dough, and repeat. Remember to scrape down the side of the bowl periodically during both stages of adding the butter and sugar. Once you cannot see any lumps of butter, the dough is ready and will be a bit softer and more glossy and elastic than before. Place the dough into a large bowl that has been lightly greased, cover and place in the fridge for a minimum of 2 hours. The longer the dough is left at this stage, the better, so overnight is best. Resting the dough helps to develop the flavours and makes it much easier to work with.

Take the brioche dough out of the fridge and tip onto a lightly floured surface. Roll the dough out to form a rectangular shape about 4mm thick. Brush the dough with lemon juice and scatter over the lemon zest. Cover the rectangle with a thin layer of poppy seeds, then roll it tightly from the base of the rectangle all the way up until you have a brioche log resembling a Swiss roll. Cut the roll into slices of your desired thickness; we suggest 5cm. Place the rounds on a baking tray or in individual ramekins. At the bakery we use metal muffin rings to hold the shape of the rolls. Cover the whole tray with a plastic bag and leave to prove for 1-2 hours.

When your brioche buns have proved, bake for 15 to 20 minutes at 180°c. When they are done, remove from the oven and allow to cool, then mix together the icing sugar with the little bit of water and lemon juice until you have a thick but dropping consistency. Dip the top of your baked brioche bun into the glacé icing, stand upright and leave to set.

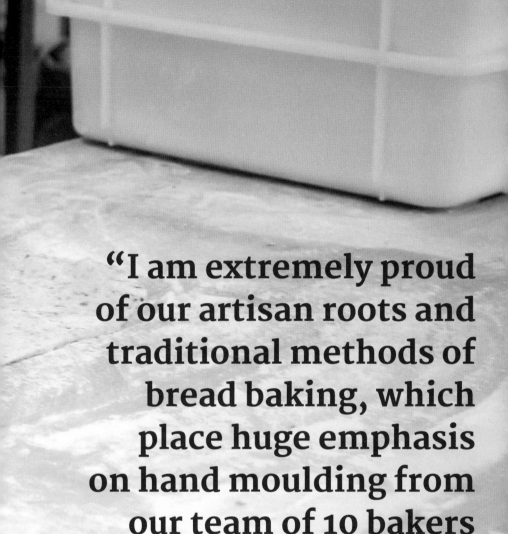

"I am extremely proud of our artisan roots and traditional methods of bread baking, which place huge emphasis on hand moulding from our team of 10 bakers who have over 100 years of baking experience between them."

Mark, general ganager, Welbeck Bakehouse

Baking
Terminology

Don't be put off by instructions to purée and zest, beat and fold your ingredients; this handy glossary explains all the usual terms used in baking so you can follow recipes from the experts with ease.

Beating

Beating involves combining ingredients quickly, either with a wooden spoon or electric whisk. It shouldn't take longer than a couple of minutes and uses much more rigorous motion than folding. The result should be a smooth mixture that hasn't curdled.

Binding

Binding usually involves adding a beaten egg (or sometimes a fat such as butter) to dry ingredients with the aim of thickening the mixture so it holds together when baked.

Blind Baking

To blind bake a pastry case, such as for a tart or flan, cover with baking paper and fill it with baking beans – these can be bought, or you can use old dried pulses instead – then bake for 10 to 15 minutes. Remove the beans and paper then bake for another 5 minutes or until the pastry is dry and just starting to colour. This is a vital step in avoiding soggy bottoms!

Combining

Combining simply describes mixing ingredients together by using either a wooden spoon or a food processor. It might also be called working, stirring or blending the ingredients together. This technique is best used when air isn't required for the mixture, such as for pastry.

Creaming

Creaming describes the process by which butter (or any dairy-free spread) and sugar are beaten together to produce a light and creamy mixture. As you combine the two ingredients with a wooden spoon or electric mixer, the colour of the mixture should lighten and the textures turn fluffy. Remember to ensure the butter is at room temperature before combining it with the sugar.

Drizzling

Drizzling is usually done in the final steps of the baking process for decoration, as well as to add flavour. It involves trickling a liquid (such as a glaze, icing or syrup) on top of the bake.

Dusting

Dusting is usually the final touch for a cake or bake. You can use icing sugar or cocoa powder to dust the top of the cake by shaking it gently through a sieve.

Folding

Folding is a technique used to incorporate light ingredients (such as whipped egg white or sifted flour) with heavier ones (such as cake mixture). The lighter ingredients should be poured over the heavier ones and the two gently combined with a metal spoon or spatula. To keep plenty of air in, use soft vertical strokes to cut down into the mixture, turning the spoon and bring it back up. Keep the bowl rotated and at a slight angle as you work, continuing the cutting and turning motion until you have a well-combined airy mixture.

Greasing and Lining

Greasing and lining a tin ensures that your cake mixture doesn't stick to the sides and bottom while it cooks, making the removal of the baked product much easier and neater. Butter the sides and base of the tin generously; you can melt and brush on the fat or use baking parchment to spread it. Greasing is usually followed by lining the tin with baking paper, which involves cutting baking paper into the correct shape to fit the base, and sides if necessary, of your tin. You don't need to grease and line when making pastry, however, as the fats in the pastry

Melting

Melting converts solid ingredients – such as chocolate or butter – to their liquid form using heat, usually in a saucepan or microwave. The best way to melt chocolate is to place a heatproof bowl over a pan of simmering water, making sure the bowl doesn't touch the water, and place the chocolate in the bowl to melt gently without risking it seizing up from overheating. This is called a bain-marie, and you might also use this method when making cheesecake or crème brûlée.

Puréeing

Puréeing smoothens or liquefies ingredients, often soft fruits, by pressing them through a sieve, or blending them in a food processor. This technique is usually used to add fruity toppings in baking.

Rubbing In

Rubbing in is a technique for combining fat – like butter or spread – and flour that's commonly used in pastry and scone recipes, to create a light and airy mixture. Place the flour and butter in a bowl, take a pinch between your fingertips and thumbs then gently rub the fat and flour together, producing a breadcrumb-like texture. Continue doing this until the fat and flour is entirely mixed together. Remember to only use your fingertips and thumbs, not your palms, because they are cooler and the idea is not to melt the fat, producing a nice short pastry or light scone as a result.

Sifting

Sifting is a method used to pass dry ingredients – usually flour, icing sugar or cocoa – through a sieve to remove any lumps. It's mostly used when making more delicate baked goods.

Simmering

Simmering is when you bring a liquid to just under boiling point over heat, usually in a saucepan on the hob. The liquid should be gently bubbling, not spitting or boiling, and at a constant temperature.

Whisking

Whisking is a method used to rapidly aerate ingredients, such as double cream or egg white. It can be done with a balloon whisk or an electric whisk, and will increase the volume of the mixture. You can whisk egg whites or double cream to a soft peak stage – when the mixture droops slightly on the whisk – or stiff peak stage – when you should be able to turn the bowl upside down without the contents falling out – depending on what the recipe calls for.

Zesting and Juicing

Zesting describes the technique of getting the zest from a skin of a fruit (usually a citrus fruit like lemons and oranges). The best way to do this is to use a really fine grater or a zester to grate the skin of the fruit. Do this over a bowl or plate to collect the zest. If you need to juice the fruit as well, do this after zesting by squeezing the cut halves over your hand or a sieve to catch any pips, or using a juicer which strains out any pulp and pips for you.

Other titles from Meze Publishing

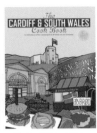

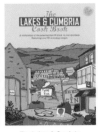

The Manchester Cook Book: Second Helpings features Ben Mounsey of Grafene, Hatch, Refuge, Masons, Old School BBQ Bus and lots more.
978-1-910863-44-2

The Cardiff & South Wales Cook Book features James Sommerin of Restaurant James Sommerin, Cocorico Patisserie, Sosban and lots more.
978-1-910863-31-2

The Cambridgeshire Cook Book: Second Helpings features Mark Abbott of Midsummer House, The Olive Grove, Elder Street Café and lots more.
978-1-910863-33-6

The Lakes & Cumbria Cook Book features Simon Rogan's L'Enclume, Forest Side, Hawkshead Relish, L'al Churrasco and lots more.
978-1-910863-30-5

The Nottingham Cook Book: Second Helpings features Welbeck Estate, Memsaab, Sauce Shop, 200 Degrees Coffee, Homeboys, Rustic Crust and lots more.
978-1-910863-27-5

The Devon Cook Book sponsored by Food Drink Devon features Simon Hulstone of The Elephant, Noel Corston, Riverford Field Kitchen and much more.
978-1-910863-24-4

The South London Cook Book features Jose Pizarro, Adam Byatt, The Alma, Piccalilli Caff, Canopy Beer, Inkspot Brewery and lots more.
978-1-910863-27-5

The Brighton & Sussex Cook Book features Steven Edwards, The Bluebird Tea Co, Isaac At, Real Patisserie, Sussex Produce Co, and lots more.
978-1-910863-22-0

The Liverpool Cook Book features Burnt Truffle, The Art School, Fraîche, Villaggio Cucina and many more.
978-1-910863-15-2

The Bristol Cook Book features Dean Edwards, Lido, Clifton Sausage, The Ox, and wines from Corks of Cotham plu lots more.
978-1-910863-14-5

The Leeds Cook Book features The Boxtree, Crafthouse, Stockdales of Yorkshire and lots more.
978-1-910863-18-3

The Cotswolds Cook Book features David Everitt-Matthias of Champignon Sauvage, Prithvi, Chef's Dozen and lots more.
978-0-9928981-9-9

The Shropshire Cook Book features Chris Burt of The Peach Tree, Old Downton Lodge, Shrewsbury Market, CSons and lots more.
978-1-910863-32-9

The Edinburgh & East Coast Cook Book features Jamie Scott from The Newport & Scott Smith from Fhior, Akva, Edinburgh Larder, Kilted Lobster and lots more.
978-1-910863-45-9

The Glasgow & West Coast Co Book features Two Fat Ladies The Gannet, Mussel Inn, Tantru Doughnuts, The Winged Ox, W Fig, Billingtons, Fruin Farm an lots more.
978-1-910863-43-5

All books in this series are available from Waterstones, Amazon and good independent bookshops.

Find out more about us at www.mezepublishing.co.uk